BY JAMES A. MICHENER

Tales of the South Pacific
The Fires of Spring
Return to Paradise
The Voice of Asia
The Bridges at Toko-Ri
Sayonara
The Floating World
The Bridge at Andau
Hawaii
Report of the County Chairman
Caravans
The Source
Iberia
Presidential Lottery
The Quality of Life
Kent State: What Happened and Why
The Drifters
A Michener Miscellany: 1950–1970
Centennial
Sports in America
Chesapeake
The Covenant
Space
Poland
Texas
Legacy
Alaska
Journey
Caribbean
The Eagle and the Raven
Pilgrimage
The Novel
James A. Michener's Writer's Handbook
Mexico
Creatures of the Kingdom
Recessional
Miracle in Seville
This Noble Land: My Vision for America
The World Is My Home

WITH A. GROVE DAY
Rascals in Paradise

WITH JOHN KINGS
Six Days in Havana

PRESIDENTIAL LOTTERY

PRESIDENTIAL LOTTERY

THE RECKLESS GAMBLE
IN OUR ELECTORAL SYSTEM

JAMES A. MICHENER

THE DIAL PRESS

NEW YORK

To
John C. Calhoun

His fierce integrity was an inspiration
His wrongheadedness, a lesson

INTRODUCTION

Steve Berry

I grew up in the 1960s, a time when the extent of reading material for kids was, to say the least, limited. R. L. Stine, J. K. Rowling, Suzanne Collins, and so many others had yet to come along. In fact, what we now know as the young adult genre had yet to be invented. Back then, at least for me, it was Hardy Boys and Nancy Drew. A limited selection, but what gems those tales were—each loaded with action, adventure, secrets, and conspiracies. Wondrous stories to fuel young imaginations. I devoured them.

Then one day when I was sixteen years old, a friend handed me a dog-eared paperback copy of *Hawaii* by James Michener. Its thousand pages immediately intimidated me, as did the small print. I'd never seen so much information packed into one book. The opening sentence alone contained thirty-six words—monstrous in comparison to the prose of Franklin W. Dixon.

But what a sentence: *Millions upon millions of years ago, when the continents were already formed and the principal features of the earth had been decided, there existed, then as now, one aspect of the world that dwarfed all others.*

I kept reading.

What unfolded was a saga spanning many centuries that described how a tiny group of islands in the Pacific Ocean were formed by nature and then settled by man. The epic involved Polynesians, Chinese, Japanese, Europeans, and Americans. Its massive chapters, hundreds of pages long, featured one expansive episode after another—each intertwined—forming a chronicle that defined both the land and its culture. I read it cover to cover. Then I found more books by this guy Michener and read every one. Eventually, I started collecting them, and now, more than forty years later, I own a first edition of each, save one—*Tales of the South Pacific*. That book is hard to find. Only a few thousand were printed and, if by some miracle one of those 1947 first editions can be found, the price is through the roof. I keep every one of my Michener books prominently displayed, wrapped in plastic. I see them every day. They are a source of pride and comfort. Today, I write modern-day thrillers in which history plays a central role. Without question, the seed for that technique was planted the day I discovered *Hawaii.*

James Michener led an incredible life. Born in 1907, he was orphaned but was soon adopted by a woman named Mabel Michener, who was already raising two other children. Some of his biographers have hypothesized that he was actually Mabel's natural son, the adoption story used to protect both of their reputations. No one knows the truth, and as an adult Michener refused to comment on the subject.

By the time he turned ten, the family had moved to Bucks County, Pennsylvania. They were poor, barely able to put food on the table. His classmates, and even a teacher or two, tormented Michener about the secondhand clothes and toeless sneakers he wore every day. Later in life he recounted that taunting with a sly smile and a twinkle in his eye. He would say that those early years instilled in him an appreciation for life that he never forgot. They taught him about living simply and not attaching too much value to material things. And though he eventually earned hundreds of millions of dollars from writing, he always feared ending up poor.

Before he'd even reached twenty years of age, Michener had traveled across the country in boxcars, by thumbing rides, or simply by walking. He worked in carnival shows and other odd jobs, and he visited all but three states. Of that time, he wrote in his 1991 autobiography, *The World Is My Home,* "Those were years of wonder and enchantment. Some of the best years I would know. I kept meeting American citizens of all levels who took me into their cars, their confidence and often their homes." He would also say that those wandering years spurred inside him an insatiable curiosity about people, cultures, and faraway lands.

In 1925 he entered Swarthmore College, a prestigious Quaker institution, on a four-year scholarship, graduating with highest honors. He attended graduate school in Scotland, then returned home and taught at a school in Bucks County. He eventually ended up in New York City, editing textbooks at Macmillan Publishing.

World War II changed everything. At age forty Michener enlisted in the navy, where he discovered the enchanting South Pacific. He earned the rank of lieutenant commander and was made a naval historian, assigned to investigate cultural problems on the various islands. A near-fatal crash landing in French New Caledonia altered the course of his life. He wrote in his autobiography, "As the stars came out and I could see the low mountains I had escaped, I swore: 'I'm going to live the rest of my life as if I were a great man.' And despite the terrible braggadocio of those words, I understood precisely what I meant."

That brush with death also made him realize what every soldier was experiencing during the war, and that one day, when the danger had passed, people might want to recall those things. So each night he began writing down observations, recording comments, describing people and places. Fifty years later, in 1991, he said:

> Sitting there in the darkness, illuminated only by the flickering lamplight, I visualized the aviation scenes in which I had participated, the landing beaches I'd seen, the remote outposts, the exquisite islands with bending palms, and especially the valiant people I'd known: the French planters, the Australian coast watchers, the Navy nurses, the Tonkinese laborers, the ordinary sailors and soldiers who were doing the work, and the primitive natives to whose jungle fastnesses I had traveled.

All of that became *Tales of the South Pacific.*

The story of how that first manuscript made it to print is typical Michener—an unexpected combination of skill, determination, and luck. Using a pseudonym, he submitted the work to Macmillan, the publisher he'd worked for before enlisting. He omitted his name because he knew the company had a strict policy against publishing anything by an employee. Once the war was over he definitely intended to return to work there, but at the time of the submission he was technically a naval officer and not an employee. So the company bought the book, which was published in 1947. One year later *Tales of the South Pacific* won the Pulitzer Prize for fiction.

Michener changed publishers in 1949, moving to Random House, where he stayed for the rest of his life. More books followed—*The Fires of Spring, Return to Paradise, The Bridges at Toko-Ri,* and *Sayonara.* Also in 1949 he moved to Honolulu and soon began work on his most ambitious project to date. Four years of research and three years of writing were needed to produce *Hawaii.* Its epic scope, length, and breadth proved to be the stamp of Michener's trademark style, one he would master over the next forty years. Legend has it that he finished *Hawaii* on March 18, 1959, the day Congress voted to accept the islands as the fiftieth state.

In 1962 Michener ran for Congress as a liberal Democrat but lost. Then, in 1968, he worked as secretary of the Pennsylvania Constitutional Convention. Outer space was a lifelong interest, and he served on NASA's advisory council, an experience that led to his novel *Space.*

Honors were something Michener shied away from, but in 1977 Gerald Ford bestowed upon him the Presidential Medal of Freedom, the nation's highest civilian award. Eventually, he wrote nearly fifty books, including five on Japanese art. His work has been translated into multiple languages, and there are more than 75 million copies of his books in print. These latest editions, being rereleased with new covers, will only add to that already staggering inventory.

A myth associated with Michener speaks of his cadre of researchers, used to gather the enormous amount of historical detail included in each of his epics. The reality was quite different. Most of the work was accomplished with the help of only three secretaries. He was a disciplined writer, establishing a routine early in his career and maintaining it his entire life. An early riser, he would go straight to work, where he wrote using a manual typewriter. He then had a light breakfast, maybe a meeting or two, and went back to work until around one P.M. Evenings were a time to be by himself. In the final year of his life, at age ninety, he still kept to his daily routine, except he spent three days a week at a renal treatment center, undergoing kidney dialysis.

The treatment proved painful in a multitude of ways, perhaps the most difficult being that it prevented him from straying far from home. The man who'd visited nearly every country could no longer travel. He told an interviewer at the time, "I sit in the TV room and see shows on the big ships I used to travel or areas that I used to wander, and a tear comes to my eye. It's not easy."

And that explains his death—he simply decided there would be no more dialysis. Instead, he welcomed the end.

Michener died on October 16, 1997.

I recall the day vividly. A segment on the evening news reported that he was gone. A sadness came over me, as if I'd lost a close friend—which, in a sense, I had.

In preparation for writing this introduction, I reviewed many articles written just after Michener passed. Most came from folks who'd had some personal contact with him through the years—an experience that had clearly stuck in their memory. All of them recounted what happened as if they had been in the presence of a king or head of state. It seemed a privilege to have spent just a little time with James Michener.

And that legacy lives on.

Though he was known to be fanatically frugal, he gave away more than $100 million. Recipients of his generosity included libraries, museums, and universities. He donated $30 million to the University of Texas for the establishment of a creative writing program. Several million more went to the creation of the James A. Michener Art Museum in Pennsylvania. One wing of that building was named for his third wife, Mari Sabusawa Michener, who died before him, in 1994.

He never really liked talking about himself, and he could frustrate interviewers. "Famous is a word I never use," he would say. "I'm well known. I've written thirty or forty books. I've done a great deal. I let it go at that." He was extremely generous with his autograph, so much so that he once noted, "The most valuable books are those that aren't signed."

Of my own collection, only one bears his signature.

To the frequently asked question, "Which book are you most proud of?" he would just smile and say, "The one I'm working on next."

By no means was he perfect. He could be a difficult man to know. He wasn't the type to start conversations with strangers, and he detested small talk. He had few close friends, and those who counted themselves in that number knew to tread lightly. He could be abrupt, even rude, and quite aloof. After his death we learned that he utilized collaborators on some of the big books, a fact he refused to acknowledge in life. He was married three times and at one point maintained a mistress. He was a multimillionaire, yet he would constantly fret about not having enough money to pay his bills. And though he was an orphan himself and a co-founder of an adoption agency, in the 1950s he gave up his claim to an adopted child when he divorced his second wife.

All of which shows that he was human.

But still, what a remarkable man.

Michener possessed an incomparable ability to simultaneously enthrall, entertain, and inform. Nobody else could write a two-hundred-word sentence with such grace and style. And he chose his subjects with great care: the South Pacific (*Tales of the South Pacific, Return to Paradise*), Judaism (*The Source*), South Africa (*The Covenant*), the West Indies (*Caribbean*), the American West (*Centennial*), the Chesapeake Bay (*Chesapeake*), *Texas, Alaska,* Spain (*Iberia*), *Mexico, Poland,* the Far East.

Like millions of other readers, I loved them all.

I never met James Michener. I would have loved to tell him how he sparked the imagination of a sixteen-year-old boy, which led first to a lifelong love of reading, then to a career as a writer. When, in 1990, I decided to write my first novel, it was Michener who influenced me most. By the end of that decade, though, changes had firmly begun to take hold. Today you won't encounter many two-hundred-word sentences or millennia-long sagas involving hundreds of characters. Instead, in the twenty-first century, story, prose, and purpose are expected to be tight. In the Internet age—with video games, twenty-four-hour news, streaming movies, you name it—there is just little time for thousand-page epics. Toward the end of his life Michener gave an interview in which he doubted he would have ever been published if he'd first started in that environment.

Thank goodness he came along when he did.

Now his stories can live forever.

CONTENTS

PRESIDENTIAL LOTTERY

THE AVERTED CHAOS

O N ELECTION DAY 1968 THE UNITED STATES ONCE AGAIN played a reckless game with its destiny. Acting as if we were immune to catastrophe, we conducted one more Presidential election in accordance with rules that are outmoded and inane. This time we were lucky. Next time we might not be. Next time we could wreck our country.

The dangerous game we play is this. We preserve a system of electing a President which contains so many built-in pitfalls that sooner or later it is bound to destroy us. The system has three major weaknesses. It places the legal responsibility for choosing a President in the hands of an Electoral College, whose members no one knows and who are not bound to vote the way their state votes. If the Electoral College does not produce a majority vote for some candidate, the election is thrown into the House of Representatives, where anything can happen. And it is quite possible that the man who wins the largest popular vote across the nation will not be chosen President, with all the turmoil that this might cause.

In 1823 Thomas Jefferson, who as we shall see had long and painful experience with this incredible system, described it as, "The most dangerous blot on our Constitution, and one which some unlucky chance will some day hit." Today the danger is more grave than when Jefferson put his finger on it.

To understand how ridiculous our system is I invite you to follow my adventures last autumn and to see for yourself how close our nation came to turmoil, if not actual disaster.

In late August my phone rang and a voice I knew well and favorably asked, "Michener, you want to be a Presidential elector?"

It was Milt Berkes, Democratic chairman for my home county, representative in the Pennsylvania lower house, and the hardest-working politician I know. When I ran for Congress, Milt was my campaign manager, and later when I was required to introduce him at public meetings I said, "Milt used my money to learn about politics. He used his own to get elected." Our friendship had gone beyond politics, for I liked this former Philadelphia schoolteacher who had moved out to the suburbs to make a good life for his family.

"Well, how about it?" he asked.

At the moment I was sick in spirit over the debacle at Chicago and wanted no involvement with politics, but as a historian and as one who had worked hard in the practical politics of Pennsylvania, I sensed that the 1968 election was going to be of special significance. . I therefore agreed to serve, even though I knew that I was heading for a potential confrontation of grave consequence.

I make this statement carefully and conscientiously: When I accepted the nomination I already knew what might happen in the fall election and I was aware of the part I could be forced to play if Pennsylvania went Democratic and thrust me into the Electoral College. Nevertheless I replied, "Sure."

All across America similar phone calls were being made. "Hey, Joe! You wanna be an elector?" "Sure, why not?"

It was as simple as that. Men and women were being chosen for one of the potentially most complex responsibilities in our political life simply because they had contributed money to the party, or had been loyal ward leaders, or were known as reliable party hacks.

If you look in Appendix A, at Article II of the United States Constitution, Section 1, paragraph 2, you will see that it says: "Each State shall appoint, in such Manner as the Legislature thereof may direct, a Number of Electors, equal to the whole Number of Senators and Representatives to which the State may be entitled in the Congress."

There are three steps in the process of becoming a duly elected elector—nomination; pledge to vote the way the state has voted; November election—and the fifty state legislatures have come up with a variety of alternatives for each.

Nomination. If one took into account the various refinements in this process he would end with a group of startling variations, but they would tend to cluster around certain agreed-upon procedures. In many states conventions of the party nominate (*e.g.,* California, Ohio). In other states the state committee chooses (Georgia, New York). In one the electors are nominated by a small executive committee (District of Columbia). Some states do not nominate but choose by state primary (Arizona, Alabama). In one state electors may be chosen "in any manner prescribed by the by-laws of the party" (Alaska). In another the governor of the state nominates, on recommendation of the political parties (Florida). In one a variety of alternatives is offered (Kentucky). In one each party may nominate two groups, one pledged, the other unpledged, and these compete in a primary (Mississippi). And in my state, Pennsylvania, the Presidential candidates chosen by the national conventions are required to name the specific electors they want to vote for them in the Electoral College if their party carries the state in November.

Pledge to vote the way the state has voted. Here again the practices vary. Some states require pledges; others do not. Some claim that a pledge has been presumed when a man offers his name in the primary of his party; others require a signed document. One official summary of the variations concludes, "In Pennsylvania, where electors are nominated by the Presidential nominee, it seems apparent that such electors must have pledged their loyalty to such Presidential nominee or he would not have selected them."

Actual election. In this area there are fewer variations. Most states do not list the names of the electors of each party on the ballot but agree that a vote for the President and Vice-President will be automatically interpreted to mean one vote for each of the allotted electors (*e.g.,* Colorado, Wisconsin). Other states print the names of the electors on their ballots (Idaho, North Dakota). In two states ballots are provided with lists of pledged and unpledged would-be electors (Alabama, Mississippi). And in one the individual parties are given discretionary choice as to whether they want the names of their electors on the ballot (South Carolina).

In addition to the above variations in procedure, the individual states also give their electors special instructions, whose terms vary enormously, but Oklahoma's is unique: "Any person elected as Presidential elector . . . after taking and filing the oath or affirmation prescribed . . . who violates said oath or affirmation by either failing to cast his ballot [for his party's candidates for President and Vice-President] or by casting his ballot for any other person shall be guilty of a misdemeanor, and upon conviction thereof shall be punished by a fine of not more than $1,000." Because this question will become important later, it should be explained now that whereas Oklahoma could quite properly fine any errant elector up to $1,000, it could not compel him to vote right in the first place, nor could the wrong vote, once cast, be corrected. States may cajole (Massachusetts) or exhort (Nevada) or threaten (New Mexico) or fine (Oklahoma) but they cannot force the elector to vote in any way other than in accordance with the dictates of his conscience—or the terms of whatever deal he may have arranged. Once he is officially and legally elected to his position, he can do what he likes, and no one can stop him in advance, even though he might be punished later. Specifically, there is no provision for a writ of mandamus, and if one were issued, it could not be enforced.

The qualified elector, therefore, is free to vote precisely as he wishes, which was the original intent of the Constitution and which is its intent now. Look at the experience in recent years.

In 1948 Preston Parks of Tennessee happened to be nominated as an elector on two different slates, one for Truman, the other for Thurmond. Truman carried the state, but Parks decided that he preferred Thurmond and voted for him. Tennessee was powerless to prevent him from doing so, for he was a legally elected Presidential elector and could do as he pleased.

In 1956 W. F. Turner of Alabama was elected to vote for Adlai Stevenson, but when the time came to vote he cast his ballot for a local judge, Walter E. Jones. In explanation Turner said, "I have fulfilled my obligation to the people of Alabama. I'm talking about the white people."

Oklahoma's law punishing such behavior came about in this way: In 1960 Henry D. Irwin, pledged to Nixon, decided to strike out on his own and cast his ballot for Senator Harry Byrd. This caused a storm of protest, but Irwin explained that in his opinion the Founding Fathers of our nation were landowners and propertied people who never intended that "the indigent, the non-property owners should have a vote in such a momentous decision" as the election of a President. Shortly thereafter Oklahoma established the requirement that a nominee elector must subscribe to a statutory oath that if elected he will cast his ballot for his party's candidate, or be liable to the $1,000 fine.

Actually, in the elections between 1820 and 1964 a total of 15,245 citizens served as electors and only four voted contrary to the will of their states. (A larger figure is sometimes cited, depending upon definitions.) The national attitude on this point was expressed vigorously by an outraged Pennsylvania voter in 1796. The state had gone for John Adams, but one of the electors decided on his own to vote for Thomas Jefferson. "Do I choose Samuel Miles to determine for me whether John Adams or Thomas Jefferson shall be President? No! I choose him to act, not to think." In general, electors have acted and not thought, but this does not establish a rule that they must always do so. The fact that this system is open to violent abuse is indeed an invitation to abuse.

In my case I was chosen to be an elector because I had worked hard for my party. I was passed upon by no public hearing, no primary vote, no board of qualifications, no review of my prior public service. My finest credentials were that each year I contributed what money I could to the party.

As to the offering of any pledge that I would vote the way my state voted, the official document previously cited surmised that since Hubert H. Humphrey, the nominee of the Democratic party, had personally chosen me as required by Pennsylvania law, it seemed "apparent that such electors must have pledged their loyalty to such Presidential nominee or he would not have selected them." This assumption is wrong on two counts. Hubert Humphrey did not nominate me, no matter what the law provided; Milt Berkes did. And no pledge of any kind was required, either verbal or written, and none was given.

I can say further that up to the convening of the Electoral College on December 16, 1968, I did not know the name of one elector from Pennsylvania, on either the Republican side or the Democratic. (I did tell one audience that I knew one of the Democratic electors, Philip Berman, an Allentown businessman of sturdy reputation, but I was wrong. It was his wife who had been chosen.)

I doubt if the voters in any state knew who the proposed electors of their party were, or cared. Electors have properly been termed "the faceless men," and in any normal year it is appropriate that they remain so; but in an abnormal year their capacity to wreck our system is so tremendous that attention must be paid them.

OCTOBER

In late August any prospect that I might be an elector was remote, because then it seemed that the Democrats had no chance of winning the nation and less of taking Pennsylvania. Although I continued to worry about the general deficiencies of the Electoral College, I did so in an impersonal way, for they no longer involved me.

In September my chances diminished, because my home district happened to include a strong concentration of Wallace supporters and it seemed possible that Wallace and not Humphrey would wind up in second place, a fear that was enhanced when the straw vote in our local high school showed Nixon winning but with Wallace pressing him in second position. Humphrey finished so far behind that students who had voted for him were conspicuous and were noted unfavorably by their companions. For some time I had believed that Nixon would win with 309 electoral votes, but my first doubt came one afternoon when Mrs. Place, my tennis-playing neighbor, told us on the courts, "I'm scared. Marketing today I met eleven people I know well. They were all for Wallace. What frightens me is this time last year they were Republicans." She was the first in our area to foresee that the Wallace vote was going to hurt not the Democrats but the Republicans. She even feared that the defection might be great enough to keep Nixon from carrying Pennsylvania. So in late September I began once more to weigh seriously what might happen if Nixon did not win enough electoral votes to decide the issue on election day.

In early October things changed dramatically. I made an extended series of political speaking trips to major cities throughout Pennsylvania—places like Scranton, Wilkes-Barre, Chester, Hazelton—and it became quite apparent that if the Democratic party was dead, word of that fact had not reached the corpse. Wherever I went I was met by large crowds who wanted to talk politics, who wanted to work. At one point I spoke to seven fund-raising dinners in a row, some in strong Republican areas where in normal years our party could collect nothing, and at every one the hall was jammed, money was forthcoming, and enthusiasm was high.

After one such dinner at which four hundred more than expected had shown up, and had paid $100 a couple, I returned home and wrote, "I'm confused. Everything seems backwards. Normally a politician's intelligence tells him he can't win, but his emotions keep him hoping. In this campaign my emotions tell me our side can't win, but my intelligence tells me that if so many people come out night after night, we've got to carry Pennsylvania and maybe even New York. There's a strong chance that Nixon is not going to get his 270 electoral votes."

In late October it became obvious that Humphrey would carry Pennsylvania and probable that Nixon would not get the majority required to win. Thus I would be a Democratic elector in precisely the kind of impasse I had feared. I spent many hours contemplating what I ought to do as a Democratic elector if the November 5 results did prove inconclusive.

Obviously, what I ought to do is what I had been nominated to do, cast an automatic vote for my party, throw the election into the House, and trust that fancy footwork among the Congressmen would enable us to salvage there the victory that had been denied us at the ballot box.

But this was not going to be a year for automatic votes, one way or the other, and I hope the reader will follow carefully what I am about to say, consulting frequently the table of election results given in Appendix D.

The significance of a deadlocked election was unavoidably clear to me, living as I did among strong Wallace supporters. If Wallace carried Alabama (10), Arkansas (6), Florida (14), Georgia (12), Louisiana (10), Mississippi (7) and South Carolina (8), he would have a total of 67 electoral votes, and this could give him the balance of power in the election, because when the Electoral College met he could direct his electors to vote not for him but for either Nixon or Humphrey, whichever would promise him the most. One man— a small, clever, intelligent rabble-rousing judge from Alabama— could determine the destiny of this nation. It was not an attractive prospect.

We must now try to determine whether this threat was real or not.

As to the risk that the election on November 5 might prove inconclusive, there could be no doubt; I feared it and so did everyone else who appreciated the possibilities. That Governor Wallace might wind up with a sizable block of votes which he could throw either way was probable. That Wallace could exercise any leverage if the election were thrown into the House seemed unlikely, in that no candidates for the House were running on the Wallace ticket nor were any publicly pledged to him; the decision there could be made apart from Wallace, so if he wished to exercise definitive leverage he had to do it promptly and in the Electoral College. Finally, since electors could do anything they pleased, and since Wallace would have a strong hold on his, I had to conclude that the Wallace threat was real, it was legal, and it could be accomplished. George Wallace could actually dictate who our President was to be. Furthermore, he had given adequate warning of his intentions.

As early as May, 1967, he had outlined his Presidential strategy in an interview with the *Richmond News*: "I might not have any chance in the House. But before you go to the House you go to the Electoral College. If we held the balance of power, we may decide the question in the Electoral College because one party may have to make a concession to the people of our country, a solemn covenant to them." Wallace went on to explain that he had used the phrase "solemn covenant" because "the word *deal* doesn't sound too good."

"Godamightydamn!" Wallace cried later. "Wouldn't it be sump'n if we win?" In Pittsburgh he spelled out the covenant that he would offer Nixon and Humphrey, if he succeeded in drawing off enough votes to wield a balance of power. Some of his ideas were reasonable, such as insistence on a better enforcement of laws; most were extraordinary, such as the abandonment of any type of civil rights legislation.

Ed Ewing, a top Wallace aide, explained how the covenant was to work. Each man or woman across the nation nominated by Wallace to stand as one of his electors would sign a notarized affidavit that he would vote, not the way his state voted, but the way Governor Wallace directed him to vote. With these pledged votes that could be swung either to Nixon or Humphrey, Wallace could go to those candidates and ask, "What will you give me if I make you President?"

Ewing pointed out that this was perfectly legal, because of our fifty states, only sixteen had laws requiring their electors to vote the way their state voted, and not one of these was a state where Wallace was likely to win. Furthermore, as we have seen, the laws were probably unconstitutional. "And anyway," Ewing added, "there's not much they could do after the fact."

Would Wallace's daring plan have worked? Both Nixon and Humphrey volunteered that they would not accept a deal with Wallace. However, Professor James C. Kirby, Jr., of Northwestern University, a leading authority on electoral reform, pointed out, "Such promises are good intentions which may more easily be stated in August than honored in November. The major candidate who was otherwise certain to lose in the House would be under tremendous pressure to negotiate with Wallace."

In early September, when it had looked as if the Republicans would easily gain control of the House, so that if a close electoral vote did develop, Nixon would be assured of election by the new House, my Republican friends told me, "Nixon would never make a deal with Wallace, but Humphrey might." In late October, when it seemed likely that the Democrats were going to retain control of the House, my Democratic friends told me, "Humphrey will never surrender to Wallace, but Nixon might."

My own conclusion was that in the forty days between the popular vote on November 5 and the electoral vote on December 16, pressures would become so tremendous and the stakes so compelling—the Presidency of the most powerful functioning democracy on earth, with all the prerogatives that position entails—that any man or party might be tempted beyond the breaking point. I expected a deal.

In what I say next I speak only for myself, but I understand that other electors, both Republican and Democratic, were of similar mind. I found the idea of permitting one man to dictate who our next President should be so repugnant, even though it was legal, that I spent some time in late October tracking down a newspaper article I remembered having read prior to the conventions. I found it. It referred to a joint statement made on July 17, 1968, by Representatives Charles E. Goodell, Republican of New York, and Morris K. Udall, Democrat of Arizona. They proposed that the two major parties agree, in the event of the election's being thrown into the House, that congressmen would pledge to vote for whichever candidate had won the popular vote, thus nullifying Wallace's capacity to dictate the election. It was a good plan, an honorable one, a plan that would have risen to the occasion of a national crisis.

But observe that Governor Wallace had anticipated just such a move; he intended not to let the election reach the House. He intended to settle the matter his own way in the Electoral College. And I intended to forestall him . . . also in the Electoral College.

As soon as it became certain that Nixon had failed to win the required 270 electoral votes, and when it was known that the election was therefore vulnerable to dictatorship by Wallace, I intended to inform all Republican and Democratic electors that I was interested in a plan whereby we would decide the election in the College between Nixon and Humphrey and not risk domination by Wallace. Rather than allow one man to dictate who our President should be, I thought it better for the nation that the two parties decide between themselves what an honorable compromise might be and then encourage their Electoral College members to swing enough votes to either Nixon or Humphrey to secure his election.

I realize the gravity of what I have just said, and I realized it at the time. I was proposing to install my judgment over tradition, and no man who knows history ever does that lightly. I was impelled by three clear motives. First, what I proposed was legal. There was absolutely nothing in law that forbade the maneuver I intended; indeed, the founders of our nation had expected that electors would behave precisely as I was proposing and only custom had developed a plan calling for their automatic subservience. Second, I was in no way personally pledged to any course of action, either by written oath, or spoken, or implied. I was as free an agent as a man could be. The Constitution required me only to act in conformance to its laws and my own good judgment, and this I proposed to do. Third, I was a loyal Democrat who had spoken till his voice was hoarse in defense of Humphrey when others had deserted him, and I had done my part in helping to keep Pennsylvania in the Democratic column. I was totally committed to a Democratic victory and I knew that if we could somehow wangle the election into the House we had a chance of winning there, but I also knew that Governor Wallace would do everything he could to forestall that; the chances of the election's going to the House were remote and probably nonexistent.

I was fortified in my conclusions by a conviction that grew each day: if I was able to see this problem so clearly, others of like mind must be seeing it too. I was convinced that across the nation potential electors in every state were weighing the same alternatives that I was and were reaching the same conclusions. If, as seemed unlikely, Humphrey were to win the popular vote and lead in the Electoral College vote, I felt certain that Republican electors would prefer to see their party and mine settle this matter between ourselves rather than subject our candidates to the pressures that Governor Wallace might apply.

I did not then communicate my ideas to any other potential elector, for three reasons. First, I knew who none of them were, and there would be ample time following the election to make my intentions known. Second, were the November 5 election to prove inconclusive, I judged that newspapers, television, magazines, and other agencies of opinion would themselves launch the kind of program I proposed, and that communication among the electors would surely be constant and overpowering. Third, if you look at the canceled parts of Article II of the Constitution you will see that an early and abiding principle of the electoral system was that the electors must not meet at one central location, but "shall meet in their respective states," the intention as stated in the debates being that this would prevent "cabal, intrigue, and corruption." When this article was superseded by the Twelfth Amendment, the prohibition was repeated in the opening sentence, and I judged that this might be interpreted to mean that correspondence between the electors was also prohibited, and if conducted, would void any plan of cooperation between the parties. At any rate, I knew what I was going to do, and I hoped that other electors of similar persuasion knew what they were going to do, also.

An overriding question haunted me then and now. Was what I proposed in any way unethical? Theoretically I had been chosen by Hubert Humphrey to help him win the Presidency; actually I had been nominated by Milt Berkes to help him keep the Democratic party strong, and these two obligations I proposed to respect. But I decided early that I would not be partner to any blackmail; I would not allow either myself or my party to be placed in a position in which deals had to be made of a character not consonant with our political principles. Also, I was much influenced by the Constitution and its original intentions. That I might have suffered censure or even excommunication was much in my mind, especially when our local newspaper awakened its readers to the fact that this might be a very close election; in an editorial they pointed out that Bucks County was fortunate in its possible electors in that both the Republican and the Democratic were men of proved integrity who could be relied upon to vote the way the state had voted. At the moment the editorial appeared I was a man prepared to do exactly the opposite, impelled by my dedication to the principles of our government and my desire to protect them.

What was it I proposed to do? If Nixon won the popular vote and led in electoral votes by a clear margin, I would recommend to my party leadership that they arrange a compromise with the Republicans and direct enough Democratic electors to swing to the Republican column to ensure Nixon's election; I would volunteer to be a member of that group and to absorb whatever opprobrium fell upon us. If the Democratic leadership showed no interest in trying to achieve such a compromise with the Republicans, I would have been willing to try myself, backed up by the electors who I felt sure would feel as I did. If such a plan were achieved, I would vote in accordance with it. If Humphrey clearly won the popular vote and the electoral votes to go with it, I would propose that the Republican high command meet with the Democratic to work out a compromise, and when it was defined, direct enough of their electors to vote for Humphrey to elect him. If they refused to do this, I would have campaigned among the Republican electors to encourage them to do so on their own account.

Finally, what do I mean by compromise? I mean just what this word has always meant in American politics since the days of the Constitutional Convention and the towering speeches of Henry Clay. I mean that if the Democratic party had ensured the election of Nixon, the Democratic party would have gained in return certain considerations as to Cabinet positions and a voice in the running of the Departments of State and Defense. I mean that if the Republicans had helped elect Humphrey, they would have been entitled to the same considerations.

The question naturally arises, "Why was this kind of compromise permissible and the Wallace covenant not?" Two answers suffice. First, the provisions of any compromise which the two major parties might have worked out would have been in the great tradition of western democracy, according to which, for example, Franklin Roosevelt brought Republicans into his wartime Cabinet and Winston Churchill brought Labour into his. If our major parties do not know where the boundaries of decency and acceptance are, then we are already lost, so I must trust them. Governor Wallace's proposals, on the other hand, were outside the traditions of our country and might have destroyed it through dictatorship or rebellion. Second, I believe that if a social organism is threatened with destruction, it has every right to defend itself. Stated bluntly, if Wallace intended to play the game he said he was playing, I intended to beat him to the punch.

ELECTION

Those who were with me on election night know with what apprehension I followed the returns. Connecticut was the first test case. If it went Republican, as many predicted, then the collapse of the Democratic party, which others had foretold, would be under way. Connecticut stood firm. It was going to be an election and not a rout.

It was quickly apparent that the popular vote was going to be extremely close; at many points Humphrey led, and my restated conviction that Nixon would win with 309 electoral votes seemed ridiculous. Fairly early in the evening Pennsylvania went definitely Democratic, so that I was an elector.

But then the long hell of the night commenced. New Jersey was lost, inexplicably, for it should have gone to Humphrey. Texas appeared to be safe for the Democrats, and at two in the morning most experts were predicting that the election would go to the House, for it looked as if California would swing to Humphrey.

With each step closer to an inconclusive election I felt more anxiety, because the very alignments I had foreseen were coming into being. The only surprise was Wallace's unexpectedly poor showing. I went to bed suspecting that the election would be deadlocked and that the contingencies I had been speculating upon would happen. The electors, that group of faceless men, would waken to find themselves at the center of a hurricane. Desolate in spirit I tried to sleep but could not, appalled that our democracy had allowed itself to fall into such a calamity when its avoidance would have been so simple. I swore then that whatever the result this new day brought, I would do what I could to abolish this ridiculous and unnecessary anachronism, for I saw then that the Electoral College serves no possible purpose except to invite the very kind of insecurity in which we were then embroiled. Any system which accidentally condones such a situation is immoral, but one which actively invites it is idiotic.

I awoke at six, with the results still not determined and with the possibility of a deadlock strong. I was then assailed by the most contradictory reactions. On the one hand I hoped that Humphrey would win enough votes to throw the election into the House, if only to prove to the nation what a gallant fighter he had been and to rebuke those experts who had laughed at his chances of victory; on the other I realized that if he did manage to force a deadlock, the popular vote and electoral, too, would be so conspicuously in favor of Nixon that it was illogical to hope for the anguish and confusion that would follow. For technical reasons which I shall discuss shortly, it seemed likely that Nixon would win in the end, so that it might be better if he won now. I truly did not know what a sensible man ought to hope for at this juncture, but as the vote in Missouri, Illinois, and California clarified, I had a sense of deep relief in knowing that an abyss had been avoided. The plan I had devised would not be needed. Symbolically, as if I were acting for the nation, I went back to sleep reassured that the peril was past. Someone else could worry about the future.

Of course, if the election had proved inconclusive, and if Wallace had managed to engineer a deal in the College, throwing his pledged electors here or there, an appeal would likely have been taken to the Supreme Court. Similarly, if my plan had succeeded, with the two major parties agreeing to a switch of votes, it too would have been challenged. There was the further possibility that the two houses of Congress might mistakenly try to apply the election law of 1887—discussed more fully on page 59—in an effort to force electors to vote the way their states had voted; but I concluded that if I understood this law correctly, Congress would be impotent. For example, if the Wallace states adhered to the law and the ritual in certifying their electors, if the electoral votes were properly recorded and transmitted, Congress would be obligated to accept and respect those results; and if Congress in its willfulness chose to do otherwise, an appeal to the Supreme Court would almost surely mandate an acceptance of the votes as cast.

Any appeal to the Supreme Court would have entailed incalculable delays. A constitutional crisis would have developed and we might not have known until well into January whether the manipulations in the Electoral College had succeeded or not. One thing is certain. Turmoil would have developed, and any foreign power who sought an excuse for attacking our troops in Vietnam, the dollar, or our position in the free world would have had a choice opportunity in the chaos we had brought upon ourselves.

There remains the chance that in a period of grave anxiety the Court might have been bullied into going against the Constitution and the law of 1887 and devising some pretext for disqualifying either the switched Wallace votes or those resulting from the Republican-Democratic fusion plan; and this Court decision would have thrown the election into the House, with results that we shall examine next. It seems entirely probable that we would have reached January 20 without knowing whom to inaugurate as our next President. (Quite possibly the Senate, being securely Democratic, would have elected Edmund Muskie as Vice-President and he would have served well into February.)

I cannot imagine a worse way to govern a nation. I cannot imagine a plan more surely calculated than this one to produce chicanery, fraud, and uncertainty. If we persist in this reckless lottery, we deserve the anguish it must ultimately bring upon us.

On one factual point I must insist. Governor Wallace was entitled to play his dangerous game of trying to decide, by himself, who our next President should be, because our election laws encouraged him to do so. The Republican and Democratic members of the Electoral College were also entitled to try to forestall him, because our election law is so damnably inexact. If the law is not changed immediately, in 1972 someone else may place himself in position to dictate, and others, with the good of their nation at heart, will have to oppose him.

ELECTION IN THE HOUSE

If our system of electing a President were rational, one would be justified in supposing, "Since we have escaped disaster in the Electoral College, the rest of the course must be secure." Quite the contrary. If an inconclusive election does manage to scrape through the pitfalls I have just outlined, it is thrown into the House of Representatives, where abominable things can happen. The risk to the nation is no less; invitation to corruption is greater; and the general insecurity of our political life is deepened. To have these two monstrous systems back to back, so that in escaping one you are thrown into the other, is an insanity that should no longer be tolerated.

When the vote in the Electoral College discloses that a Presidential election has been inconclusive, the three candidates with the highest electoral votes move to the House of Representatives, which chooses among them. The House can, as we shall see, pass over the man with the most electoral and popular votes and choose the second or third, so that the man chosen is a minority President in every sense of the word.

This is bad enough, but the process of voting is even worse. Each of the fifty states is given one vote, with twenty-six being required for election. The disposition of a state's vote is determined by a poll of the state's delegation to the House. If the delegation has more Republicans than Democrats, the one vote would normally be cast for the Republican candidate. If the delegation is predominantly Democratic, the one vote would probably be Democratic. In case the state's delegation happens to be evenly balanced—or in case some member is ill or absent, producing a tie—that state is totally disfranchised and has no vote. Obviously, in an election in which several states had tie delegations, enough votes might be immobilized to prevent an election.

It is difficult to describe the injustices and imbalances produced by this system. Suppose a close election in the House, with the vote of each state crucial. In the fall election Alaska, with its 1968 population of 277,000, would have been entitled to only one representative, so the vote of its delegation could not possibly be tied; but California, with a population of 19,221,000, would have had 38 representatievs, and its vote might stand at 19–19. In such an instance Alaska would have one vote, and California none. Or suppose that California's delegation split 20 Republicans to 18 Democrats. Then Alaska would have one vote, and California would also have one, so that in choosing a President, Alaska would have something like sixty-nine times the leverage of California. These enormous discrepancies would be duplicated when comparing Nevada with New York, or Vermont with Pennsylvania.

In this system, 59 judiciously chosen House members representing the 26 smallest states can control the election, regardless of how 359 members from the 24 largest states vote. Using the 1960 census figures, the small 26 had a total population of only 31 million, but they could outvote the large 24 with a population of 149 million. This is minority power with a vengeance, and when the 1970 census figures apply, the discrepancies may be even greater.

Put even more bluntly, Alaska, Nevada, Wyoming, and Vermont, with a total population of about 1,467,000, according to 1968 estimates, would have four votes in choosing the President and would thus outvote California, New York, and Pennsylvania, with a population of more than 49 million, but with only three votes.

If the House system worked efficiently, we could tolerate the enormous advantage accorded the small states, and the regrettable disfranchisement of tie-vote states, but actually the system is a shambles and an invitation to fraud. Presidential elections have only twice wound up in the House, once in 1800 and again in 1824, and the performance each time was frightening. In the former year the party which later became the Democrats backed Thomas Jefferson for President and Aaron Burr for Vice-President, and this was so clearly understood that the electors did not specify which man was to hold which position, with the result that each got 73 electoral votes. Burr, a man without principle who would later be charged with betrayal of his nation, saw a chance to profit from the accidental development and grab the Presidency for himself. In a letter that was nobly worded and widely published he disclaimed any interest in that position: "It is highly improbable that I shall have an equal number of votes with Mr. Jefferson; but if such should be the result, every man who knows me ought to know that I should utterly disclaim all competition. Be assured that the Federal party can entertain no wish for such an exchange. As to my friends, they would dishonor my views, and insult my feelings by a suspicion that I could submit to be instrumental in counter-acting the wishes and expectations of the United States— and I now constitute you my proxy, to declare these sentiments if the occasion shall require."

But behind the scenes Burr worked to the opposite purpose, lining up Federalist votes for himself and encouraging all who wished to defect from Jefferson, who maintained the gentlemanly aloofness for which he was noted.

The election went to the House, where, under the rules of that day, the choice would be made between the two top contenders, Jefferson and Burr. One hundred and six representatives were eligible to vote, representing sixteen states, with nine state votes being required for election.

The balloting started on Wednesday, February 11, 1801, in a snowstorm. Two representatives were absent, and two states had deadlocked delegations. The first ballot showed Jefferson 8, Burr 6, deadlocked 2. Jefferson had failed of election by one vote, and his gleeful opponents believed they could muster enough opposition to keep him from the Presidency.

Since the inconclusive vote established on the first ballot was to maintain throughout the election, and since it could have been duplicated in principle in 1969, it will be instructive to analyze what happened:

For Jefferson: New York, New Jersey, Pennsylvania, Virginia, North Carolina, Georgia, Kentucky, Tennessee—principally southern states with the addition of three big states in the north.

For Burr: New Hampshire, Massachusetts, Rhode Island, Connecticut, Delaware, South Carolina—principally New England states plus one border and one southern.

Deadlocked: Vermont, Maryland—two accidental ties.

New Jersey's vote for Jefferson was extremely tenuous, since that state was divided three to two, with a swing man who was notoriously undependable; no one knew which way he would vote next and it was said that the New Jersey count should be recorded permanently as 2½ to 2½. The two ties were of interest in that Vermont's was due to the personal disgust her two representatives felt for each other, while Maryland was prevented from voting for Burr only by the courageous presence of a man who was so near death that he was kept in a cot off the voting chamber. A crucial question before each ballot was, "Is Joseph Nicholson still alive?"

A second vote was taken, and the results stood the same. All that night the House balloted, twenty-five times, without a change in the stubborn line-ups. The two Vermont men refused to compromise, or even to speak to each other, and Joseph Nicholson continued to rise from what all judged to be his deathbed to prevent Maryland from going to Burr.

In the cold dawn of Thursday morning it became evident that the House was not going to settle this issue at one sitting, so in direct violation of the Constitution, which required them to stay till the job was done, they recessed till eleven that morning. At that hour the same results were forthcoming, so they recessed again.

At noon on Saturday the voting resumed, with the same result: Jefferson 8, Burr 6, deadlocked 2. No President.

The twenty-eighth ballot produced the same results, as did the thirtieth and thirty-first, but as the thirty-second was called, the dramatic break that all had waited for arrived. From the North Carolina delegation a gentleman rose, and in a voice quaking with emotion, announced that it was time for principle to overcome private interest and proposed to switch his vote from Burr to Jefferson. There were cheers and huzzahs until someone pointed out that since North Carolina was already for Jefferson, the switch signified nothing. Score on the thirty-second ballot: 8–6–2, with North Carolina voting for Jefferson, as she had done thirty-one times previously. The score on the thirty-third was the same, and the delegates broke up for a recess which would carry over Sunday.

It seems extraordinary, at this distance and with what we now know, that these congressmen were so reluctant to elect Thomas Jefferson, one of the noblest minds this nation has produced, but clung to Aaron Burr, one of the most mercurial and undependable, but the bitterness with which the Burr men opposed Jefferson is proved by the stubbornness of their vote.

A great deal of politicking took place over the weekend. Certain deals were proposed and rejected. Others struck the fire of imagination and promised possibilities, which never did materialize. There was talk of rebellion; there was fear of anarchy; and on Monday the voting resumed.

The thirty-fourth ballot revealed the same obdurate lines of resistance—8–6–2—but there was a rumor that the Maryland delegation might be prepared to break its deadlock, not through the death of Joseph Nicholson, who lived through to the bitter end, but because a Burr supporter felt that this travesty could continue no longer and threatened to vote for Jefferson. (Nicholson survived till 1817 and earned a place in history because one day he saw some lines scribbled by his brother-in-law and brought them to the attention of the public on the ground that they exhibited a fine patriotic sentiment. His brother-in-law was Francis Scott Key and the poem thus saved was "The Star-Spangled Banner.")

The House, sensing that grave decisions were impending, recessed so that adversaries could consider their positions, and on Tuesday morning, February 17, 1801, when the House reconvened, there was again wild rumor that Maryland had broken its tie and would vote for Jefferson, but on the thirty-fifth ballot Maryland continued her deadlock. When the thirty-sixth ballot was called for, however, members saw with amazement that the issue had been decided for them in an unforeseen way: one of the two chairs in the Vermont delegation was empty, and it was the Burr supporter who was abstaining. His state could now vote Jefferson one, Burr none. A President had been elected. To make it certain, Burr men in Maryland also abstained, allowing that state as well to go for Jefferson. In Delaware and South Carolina the delegations were all Burr men; they agreed to withhold their votes from him but they were damned if they would vote for Jefferson, so they did not participate and their states were recorded as abstaining. Final vote: Jefferson 10, Burr 4, abstentions 2.

A major reason why the House had been able to hold the line for Jefferson through this parade of thirty-five deadlocked ballots was that Alexander Hamilton patriotically swallowed his personal hatred for Jefferson and led the fight against Burr, whom he knew to be inadequate. Said Hamilton at the beginning of the battle, "I trust the Federalists will not finally be so mad as to vote for Burr. I speak with intimate and accurate knowledge of his character. His elevation can only promote the purposes of the desperate and profligate. If there be a man in the world I ought to hate, it is Jefferson. With Burr I have always been personally well. But the public good must be paramount to every private consideration." Three years later Burr killed Hamilton in a duel, occasioned in part by the bitterness of this election.

Some historians make the point that this House election of 1801 ought not to be used as a precedent for trying to anticipate what a House election would be like in this century, because the Twelfth Amendment, which came quickly upon the heels of this disturbing performance, altered the rules to correct some of the weaknesses which the Jefferson-Burr fight disclosed. This is sound reasoning, except that the aspects of the 1801 House election which I have been stressing—the confusions that grow out of the vulnerable system of allotting each state one vote—remain the same, and to that extent the analogy is pertinent. What happened in 1801 was exactly what we could have expected in 1969.

The second House election, however, would in other respects present a closer analogy, for the constitutional rules which governed it are identical with those that operate today; of course, each new Congress draws up its own by-laws at the beginning of its biennial session, and the 91st would have done this, so that certain of the housekeeping techniques might have been altered but not the basic voting principles.

In 1824 Andrew Jackson had nearly won the Presidency outright. He led by a large margin in both the popular and electoral votes, but since four candidates had fought the election, he failed to gain an outright majority of the electoral votes. Again the House had to choose a President. This time only one ballot was required, but it was a beauty. John Quincy Adams seems to have made a deal with Henry Clay, who had wound up in fourth place, whereby Clay would throw his votes to Adams in return for the post of Secretary of State. That was how it worked out, and Jackson, robbed of an election which should have been his, fulminated, "Was there ever witnessed such a bare-faced corruption in any country before?"

When our Constitution was framed, most of the delegates appeared to agree with the estimate of George Mason of Virginia, who predicted that "19 times in 20" the final choice of the President would be made in Congress. But the results of House election have been so turbulent and untrustworthy that few today would recommend that we retain the procedure.

A bizarre weakness of the plan is that with the House electing the President and the Senate the Vice-President—in its case, choosing from the top two candidates—the two could come from different parties, which in our system could create much havoc.

It was against this background that I contemplated the possibility that the 1968 election might be thrown into the House. By mid-October there was strong likelihood that this would happen; certain polls and responsible newspapers even suggested that Wallace was going to finish in second place and Humphrey a poor third. As I have explained, I intended to do all I could to settle the issue in the Electoral College, but I saw good reason why my effort would fail. Therefore, the possibility of a House election was to be taken seriously.

I hope that at this point the reader will study carefully Appendix D and construct for himself a list of the possibilities that could have emerged on election day, to produce an inconclusive result. The simplest contingency involves Illinois and Missouri:

| | Candidate | | | Electoral |
State	Nixon	Humphrey	Difference	Vote
Illinois	2,174,774	2,039,814	134,960	26
Missouri	811,932	791,444	20,488	12

If Nixon had lost these two states, which he could have done with a swing of only 67,481 votes in Illinois and 10,245 in Missouri, he would have had not 302* electoral votes but 38 fewer, or 264, which

---

*As we shall see (pages 44, 123–126), the defection of a North Carolina elector cut Nixon's vote to 301.

would have been insufficient for him to be elected. In other words, we came very close to a House election.

Since it is traditional for the incoming Congress to hold the election, it would have been the political division of the 1969 House that would have determined whether Nixon or Humphrey would be President, so its composition must be kept in mind throughout the discussion that follows (see table below).

Since 26 states are required to elect a President, and since the 21 regular Democratic states plus the 5 southern states that went for Wallace but which have Democratic majorities would add up to that number, it might at first glance seem likely that Humphrey would have won. However, this implies several assumptions that are not necessarily valid.

Assumption 1. That the five Wallace states would vote Democratic. It is true that Wallace controlled no House members by having them as announced members of his party and running on his ticket;

Composition of the State Delegations in the 91st Congress According to

Democratic Majority			Republican Majority		
California	21 D	17 R	Alaska	0 D	1 R
Colorado	3 D	1 R	Arizona	1 D	2 R
Connecticut	4 D	2 R	Delaware	0 D	1 R
Florida	9 D	3 R	Idaho	0 D	2 R
Hawaii	2 D	0 R	Indiana	4 D	7 R
Kentucky	4 D	3 R	Iowa	2 D	5 R
Maine	2 D	0 R	Kansas	0 D	5 R
Massachusetts	7 D	5 R	Michigan	7 D	12 R
Missouri	9 D	1 R	Minnesota	3 D	5 R
Nevada	1 D	0 R	Nebraska	0 D	3 R
New Jersey	9 D	6 R	New Hampshire	0 D	2 R
New York	26 D	15 R	New Mexico	0 D	2 R
North Carolina	7 D	4 R	North Dakota	0 D	2 R
Oklahoma	4 D	2 R	Ohio	6 D	18 R
Pennsylvania	14 D	13 R	South Dakota	0 D	2 R
Rhode Island	2 D	0 R	Utah	0 D	2 R
South Carolina	5 D	1 R	Vermont	0 D	1 R
Tennessee	5 D	4 R	Wisconsin	3 D	7 R
Texas	20 D	3 R	Wyoming	0 D	1 R
Washington	5 D	2 R			
West Virginia	5 D	0 R			
Total:	**21 states**			**19 states**	

but he did control their sympathies, and there might have been enormous profits either to them personally or to their states if they voted Republican in order to deprive Humphrey of a victory. On the other hand, these southern states appreciate the advantages that accrue to them when a Democrat is in the White House and they would not lightly throw away that leverage. I doubt that one can estimate now how these states would have voted, but we do know that they would have been the focus of such dealing, such chicanery, such promises, and such log-rolling as we have not seen for a long time.

Assumption 2. That the 21 states in the Democratic column would have mustered all their delegates through twenty or thirty ballots. Kentucky, Nevada, Pennsylvania, and Tennessee would all have Democratic margins of one vote; illness or absence could immobilize these states and cast them into the deadlocked column. Of course, by the same reasoning, Republican majorities of one in the following states would have been equally vulnerable: Alaska, Arizona, Dela-

House of Representatives of the the 1968 Election

Wallace States			Delegations Deadlocked		
Alabama	5 D	3 R	Illinois	12 D	12 R
Arkansas	3 D	1 R	Maryland	4 D	4 R
Georgia	8 D	2 R	Montana	1 D	1 R
Louisiana	8 D	0 R	Oregon	2 D	2 R
Mississippi	5 D	0 R	Virginia	5 D	5 R

(Needed for election—26.)

Total:	5 states	5 states

ware, Vermont, Wyoming. It must be remembered, however, that in the early stages of the balloting the Republicans would have been in the passive posture of merely trying to prevent a Democratic victory, so that it would not have mattered if some of their states had fallen into the deadlocked column, since deadlocked states would have counted as votes against the Democrats. Of course, when it came time for the Republicans to try to put together 26 votes of their own to elect Nixon, any defection would have been fatal, but in general the possibility of deadlocked states would have hurt the Democrats more than the Republicans.

Assumption 3. That the deadlocked delegations would have remained deadlocked. The pressures on these split delegations would have been tremendous, and that they could have remained evenly balanced is doubtful. Remember that it was the unlocking of such delegations in 1801 that finally solved that impasse, and in a protracted series of indecisive ballots, it would probably again be the deadlocked delegations that would decide the issue.

Assumption 4. That Republicans would remain Republicans and Democrats stay Democrats through a long impasse. In 1801, key delegates withdrew their loyalty on the crucial ballot. This would probably have happened in 1969, too.

One can say with certainty that on the day it became clear that the 1968 election was headed to the House, a band of the most expert character analysts in the nation—the henchmen of the major parties—would have been studying each House member with a microscope, his family, his college deportment, his bank loans, his son's addiction to drugs, his business interests, in order to find the weak spots in that man's armor. And when those spots were found, a dozen prying fingers would be thrust therein to tear that man apart. It would require supermen to withstand these pressures.

In addition, there would have been the normal pressures of a troubled conscience: what ought a man who loves his country and his party do at this point? These are not light matters, but our election system seems to delight in placing men in positions where unusual and unnecessary pressures are thrust upon them.

Another factor which must be taken into account in calculating whether the apparent majority of Democratic states could have been delivered to Humphrey is the climate of opinion that would have existed at the time balloting took place. It would not have been conducive to a Humphrey victory. Television, still smarting from Chicago, would have continued to do all it could to discredit the Democrats. Its probing eye would have sought out every evidence of a break in Democratic ranks and exploded the rumor into fact. Meetings between negotiating delegates, supposed to be clandestine, would have been magnified into treachery. Newspapers which tended to support the Republican side, or did so outright, would have been justified in pointing out that since Nixon had won a plurality of the popular vote, however slight, he was entitled to the Presidency and that to deny him was treason. Gangs of young white people from the radical left would have descended on Washington to make one supreme effort to deny the Presidency to Humphrey, the inheritor of Johnson, and there would have been some ugly scenes, all reported instantly across the nation as proof of what might be expected if the Democrats won; but the solemn fact is that the election would have been conducted in the city of Washington, predominantly a Negro city, and when these citizens saw that all public pressures were being applied on the side of Nixon, a man who had ignored them in the campaign and against whom they had voted heavily (139,556 to 31,012), there would have been a great temptation to launch rallies and riots of their own, to offset what they saw happening on television. This tenseness would have been increased by the fact that whereas the Twenty-third Amendment awarded the District of Columbia three votes in the Electoral College, those votes would have been lost when the election went to the House, since the District of Columbia has no representation there. The vote would have been held in Washington, but with Washington itself excluded. Finally, the analogies that one would naturally draw between 1801 and 1969 would in one vital area not apply. Then it required days and even weeks for news of what was transpiring in Washington to reach the hinterlands; even Burr, staying in New York, was not informed until two days later at the best as to what the vote had been in crucial tests. Time and distance softened the impact; when unpleasant news did reach a distant city, what could the citizens do about it, since the fact was now history accepted by the capital? In 1969 the sharing of news is instantaneous, and if the seven days of suspense that characterized the 1801 election were to have been repeated in 1969, the anxiety would not only have been much more intense; it would also have embraced the whole nation. Because the frustration would have been instantaneous, those frustrated would have felt that they could do something about it, and I am apprehensive when I contemplate what form that action might have taken.

How would the 1969 House election have gone? The balance of power as shown in the composition of state delegations gives no cause for thinking that it would have gone easily. Theodore G. Venetoulis, in his analysis of the House election system,[*] has a grimly amusing chapter containing nineteen pages of speculation on "1968—The Year No President Was Elected." He carries his imaginary election through twenty-three deadlocked ballots, and as the capital prepares for the twenty-fourth, a snow begins to fall, as it had in a similar situation in 1801. Reading his account after the Nixon-Humphrey election, one realizes that he has not relied on fantasy. It all could have happened.

Looking at the problem of House election, Venetoulis concludes: "It is inevitable that any Presidential election thrust into the Congress is going to touch off a horrendous struggle that will strain the political ethics of our society. The Presidency of the United States must not be the product of insolent intrigue, malapportioned gimmickry, or crude coalitions fashioned out of despair, exhaustion, or blackmail."

James Madison, even though he had helped draft the Constitution, had no illusions about the error of having inconclusive elections thrown into the House. In 1823 he had unequivocal thoughts on the mistake he and his colleagues had made: "The present rule of voting for President by the House of Representatives is so great a departure from the republican principle of numerical equality, and even from the Federal rule, which qualifies the numerical by a State equality, and is so pregnant also with a mischievous tendency in practice, that an amendment to the Constitution on this point is justly called for by all its considerate and best friends."

If an amendment was needed in 1823—two years before the Jackson-Adams deadlock—how much more is one needed today. Fortunately, as we shall see, there are two quite simple escapes from this error, and each is easily attainable by amendment. First, when the electoral vote is inconclusive, a run-off election could be held immediately between the two top candidates, and this would produce a quick, final, and easily accepted solution. Second, if the nation does not want the expense and protracted anxiety of another nationwide

---

[*] *The House Shall Choose* (Elias Press, Margate, New Jersey, 1968).

election so soon after the first, the choice could be thrown into the House, but the Senate would meet with the House in joint session and each member of Congress would have one vote. Since there would be 535 members in all, 268 votes would be required for election, and the nonsense of permitting deadlocked states to have no vote at all would be ended, along with the injustice of allowing Alaska to have sixty-nine times the voting power of California.

I shall say more about these alternatives later, but with such easy solutions at hand, it is difficult to explain why we cling to a discredited procedure which might bring us much grief.

II

THE
FORTY-NINE
STEPS

EVEN THOUGH I WAS DETERMINED TO WORK FOR THE ABOLI-
tion of the Electoral College, I felt that since I was an elected
member I should treat the tradition with respect, but society con-
spired against me. Newspapers in the area conducted man-on-the-
street interviews regarding the College, and the replies were comical.

One man said, "Every boy and girl should go to college and if
they can't afford Yale or Harvard, why, Electoral is just as good, if
you work."

A woman in Philadelphia said, "I've heard some very nice things
said about Electoral. It's here in the neighborhood somewhere. I
think it's that bunch of red-brick buildings about three blocks farther
down." And she pointed toward Independence Hall.

A sporting type said, "The guys at the bar poor-mouth Electoral
somethin' awful. Wasn't they mixed up in a basketball scandal or
somethin'?"

Another man spoke for the majority. "I think every kid should go
to Electoral . . . whether they want to or not."

In the course of several weeks I interrogated about fifty of my
friends, a majority with college educations, and was surprised at the
general ignorance I encountered. Not one understood the full complexity of the system. Most were uninformed on any but the grossest

functions. And even those few who understood the principle of the College were astonished when I pointed out that as of that date, no one really knew for sure who had won the November election.

"Then why is Nixon picking a Cabinet?" was a frequent rejoinder. When I tried to explain that in order to run the system we had to take certain things for granted, I received incredulous stares the intent of which I preferred not to decipher.

What really irritated my panel, however, was my assurance that on November 5 no one—neither they nor I nor Richard Nixon—had voted for President, but only for this nameless group of electors who would later do the job for the nation. This they felt to be totally preposterous, and in certain cases I thought it best not to pursue the matter. I am sure those people remain convinced that I had it all backwards because they could remember as clear as day going into the voting booth and marking their vote for Richard Nixon. It was there on the machine in big letters and they had pulled the lever for him. I reflected that in their stubbornness they had much companionship. I would suppose that in this error they were joined by at least three quarters of our population, for our citizens would be appalled if they ever woke up to the fact that they had not voted for President.

Any system which induces such misconception is dangerous, because if in a close election the winner of the popular vote were to be deprived of the Presidency by manipulations in either the Electoral College or the House, there could be a disillusionment so vast that it might lead to large-scale disaffection or worse. And when one reflects that this risk is run on behalf of a College that is not needed and serves no creative function, the folly of retaining it becomes even more clear. It was with such gloomy speculations that I prepared to report to Harrisburg to play my role as a member of this curious institution.

On the morning of my departure a blizzard invaded the eastern part of the state, blowing in upon us from the Atlantic, and within a few hours it deposited on our roads some six inches of snow, laid down upon a foundation of ice.

Since it seemed unlikely that I would be able to reach the capital if I waited till mid-morning to depart, I rose at five and in the gloomy hour before sunrise, headed westward. Snow swirled through the darkness. The air was bitter. And gales whipped the snow into such deep drifts across our country roads that I felt certain I was going to be bogged down before I got fairly started.

Fortunately, a few farmers were out and their milk trucks had broken a trail which allowed me to reach a main road, but this headed directly into the storm, and although the road surface was cleaner, driving was even more hazardous than it had been on the back trails. My windshield was quickly caked with snowy ice, and when dawn began to break, gray and ugly and freezing, I was still only a few miles from home.

It was an unseasonable storm and therefore crippled a large area that might have been able to handle it more easily later in the winter. In the first hour I saw three cars badly disabled and concluded that I would have to turn off the road and wait till some service station opened where I could keep warm. I thought it unlikely that I would make Harrisburg.

And then I met a truck coming eastward. We both stopped, and the driver yelled, "What the hell goes on here?"

"Sudden storm."

"Storm! This damned thing's a blizzard. Look at the drifts." He left his truck and stared down the barely visible road. "How long's this been going on?"

"Five or six hours. Why? Hasn't it been snowing where you've been?"

"Hell no!"

"Where've you been?"

"Harrisburg."

When I smiled, he told me that up the road about twenty miles, at Allentown, the roads were clear. "You'll have a straight run in to Harrisburg. No trouble."

I told him he'd have plenty of trouble in the direction he was headed, and we parted. He was right. After about forty more minutes of very difficult going, with some cars stranded and others in the ditch, I at last reached the point at which the storm had stopped, a line as clear as if drawn by a pencil, and from there the road was open and clear and bitterly cold. The snow would follow later, but on that day it would not catch up with me, so within a few hours I was in my hotel room in Harrisburg.

I had been summoned a day early to meet with those officials whose duty it would be to see that the procedures on Monday moved swiftly and legally. I was not quite sure why I had been asked to participate, but a splendid old parliamentarian for the Republican party, who would supervise the proceedings and get little joy from shepherding a bunch of Democrats, explained over the telephone that the electors had been consulted and they wanted me to serve as their president. What he and I decided on Sunday would be the procedure on Monday. He would wait for me in the capitol.

I put the phone down and considered the ambivalent moral position in which I found myself. That my peers had selected me to be their president was an honor which I appreciated, for I had stood with many of them in political wars and I was pleased that together we had helped carry our state for the Democratic party. But at the same time I recalled with painful clarity the course I had decided to follow had the Presidential election proved inconclusive. In those days, as danger threatened, I had determined to subvert the Electoral College in an effort to forestall either a Republican or a Democratic deal with Governor Wallace; now, the storm having subsided, I was being asked to lead that College in the routine performance of its constitutional duties. I wondered if I had a right to accept that leadership.

I walked the short distance to the magnificent capitol building, one of the grandest and most gracious in the fifty states. I had known the building since childhood, and its history had always fascinated me, for in addition to being beautiful, this capitol was also the most infamous in American state history, winning that honor by a nose over the notorious structure in Colorado.

In 1897, while the legislature was in session, the old capitol had burned right to the ground. It must have been a fine blaze, because we had prints of it in our classroom in primary school, with agitated firemen running here and there in dashing poses and accomplishing nothing. Quickly the legislature authorized $500,000 for a replacement, but the result was appalling. "Nothing but a warehouse!" some newsman protested when he saw the finished job, and this became the accepted verdict. It was a disgrace to the commonwealth, and the legislature, properly embarrassed, had promptly voted $4,000,000 to build a real capitol.

For those days the fund was ample, and the result was noble. The halls were spacious. The rotunda dominated the countryside. And the building looked so solid and clean and stable that everyone agreed the state had got even more for its money than the plans had promised.

In this mood of euphoria the legislature reasoned: "If the people wanted us to spend not $500,000 but $4,000,000 and if they wanted not a warehouse but a granite masterpiece, they would also like to see it well furnished." So by one device or another, but principally by the trick of setting up personal companies which would sell chairs and rugs and lighting fixtures—companies which would be owned by the legislators themselves—these public servants managed to spend $9,600,000 at 1906 prices. Chairs were sold at $5,000 each. Chandeliers which were bought in New York for $40 were sold in Harrisburg for $3,000. Rugs were paid for at a rate that would have exhausted the looms of Samarkand and Bokhara, but the rugs that were delivered had been woven in Brooklyn. It was a steal of such magnitude that it set a lasting standard for the history books. "The Harrisburg capitol!" I heard again and again in my youth, and men who had sold brass spittoons at a price they would have brought if made of solid gold were pointed out to me as folk heroes, which they were, for so far as I knew then, no one connected with the vast swindle ever went to jail.

I remember when I first saw the result. It was about 1920, when the building was fourteen years old and I thirteen, and it seemed so handsomely proportioned, so ornately ornamented and with such splendid chairs and spittoons that I outraged my civics teacher by blurting out to our class, "It was worth every penny."

Now, as I approached it for serious duty, I thought of that high-domed room, still captivating to schoolchildren, where the flamboyant murals of Violet Oakley had occupied my attention on that first visit. Around the inside of the dome Miss Oakley had painted the procession of the hours, all twenty-four of them, from midnight through high noon and back to midnight in one marvelous swirl of tall and graceful ladies, those for the night hours clothed in ominous black, those for daylight mainly naked. It was quite a performance.

The Electoral College was to meet, I was told, in the Senate Chamber, one of the finest small rooms in American government, a striking symphony of gold and green and dark blue. Staring at us here would be a somber Abraham Lincoln at Gettysburg, standing under the emblazoned words which he had spoken at that battlefield on November 19, 1863: "It is for us the living rather to be dedicated to the unfinished work."

When I met with the officials I found that all was not well with the Electoral College. Of the twenty-nine Democrats elected to the membership, six had already phoned in to report that they were not going to make it to Harrisburg. That meant that we had to round up six substitutes, and this had been done by scanning the lists of men and women who held political jobs in Harrisburg, but no sooner had we adjusted the schedule so as to qualify these substitutes than a messenger arrived from Democratic headquarters with the news that two more were not going to make it. So we extended our list of substitutes to eight, choosing anyone who came to mind.

This arbitrary procedure did not surprise me, for on November 26 I had received a letter asking if I was going to bother to show up: "We have been advised by some of the Electors of their inability to serve. If you, for any reason, find you are unable to do so, we will appreciate hearing from you. A replacement will be made but this cannot be done before the time of the meeting of the Electoral College."

Of the twenty-nine Democrats who had been elected to serve in Pennsylvania, only twenty-one would be with us. Absenteeism is an occupational disease in the Electoral College. In some states criers go up and down the halls asking if anyone wants to be a Presidential elector, and those who respond are sworn on the spot and by this accident attain a critical power. In Pennsylvania we managed a little more decorum. We did have a list of names, but no one had voted on them, no one had approved them, and from this list we picked people to select a President.

In 1948, when it came time for the Republican electors of Michigan to convene in Lansing, only thirteen of the nineteen bothered to show. According to custom, officials scurried through the capitol looking for anyone who would serve, and they came upon a Mr. J. J. Levy of Royal Oak, who was duly sworn. But when it came time to vote they had much trouble with Levy, because he insisted upon casting his ballot not for Dewey and Warren, who had carried Michigan, but for Truman and Barkley, who had lost by 35,000 votes. Argued Levy, "I thought we had to vote for the winners."

I had little time to worry about the eight missing electors, for I was now handed the list of forty-nine separate steps through which we would move on Monday. I reproduce this archaic formula as Appendix E because I want the reader to appreciate the panoply that surrounds the Electoral College and to experience the emotions I did when directing the Pennsylvania electors through the ritual.

At first glance I was staggered by the complexity. Then I saw Step 22 and laughed. Then I saw Steps 38 through 41 and realized what a wealth of history and near-tragedy they summarized. Then I read the whole again, and said to myself, "What a confused set of rules contrived by men trying to control a function that is left completely without control," because not one of these forty-nine ingenious rules would in even the slightest way have prevented Governor Wallace from disrupting the larger College of which we were a part, or kept me from combating him in my own arbitrary way. Finally, I felt that deep sense of respect which any historian must feel when he comes into contact with the ritual by which a self-governing nation endeavors to safeguard its legitimacy. Complicated and foolish though these procedures may have seemed, they were the tradition of our nation and I intended supervising them with dignity, for if this was the procedure our nation had chosen, I would do what I could to ensure its respectful performance. But that night I went to bed more convinced than ever that this dangerous College, this time bomb lodged near the heart of the nation, must be abolished.

Any apprehensions I might have had about the propriety of my serving as president of the Electoral College were dissipated the next morning by an extraordinary conversation I had with one of the delegates. When I entered the capitol I heard the mellifluous voice of a giant Texan calling to me: "Michener! What in hell are you doing back at the scene of your crime?"

It was Matthew Gouger, a Texas free-wheeler who had drifted north to make a fortune in various businesses and whom I had got to know when we served together as delegates to Pennsylvania's Constitutional Convention earlier that year. He was a big man, big in speech, big in metaphor, big in spending, and big in Mississippi riverboat graciousness. At the convention I had known him for three days before I realized that he was a Democrat; by every external standard he should have been a conservative, big-hearted, and sensible Republican, but something had gone awry and he had come out of his extensive business experience a profoundly liberal Democrat. In the convention he had astonished me by the courage he displayed in taking on the established powers one after another in frontal assault. He was castigated on the floor, abused in private, and respected by everyone. I shall not soon forget how, after Matt and I had stood together on a dozen different matters, I finally put forth one that was rather close to my heart and then sat down to hear him tear it to shreds on a weakness which I had overlooked.

He was a mime, and at his copious dinner parties he used to entertain us with outrageous yarns in which various leaders appeared in ridiculous postures; he was also a professional Texan, with stories of the range that went on like the Texas horizon. I had not known that Matt Gouger was to be a member of the Electoral College, but when I saw him I felt strangely relieved. I said to myself as he started a yarn about his last trip to Texas, "If there had been a brawl in the College, Matt's the kind of man we would have needed to fight it to an honorable conclusion."

I was about to confess my apprehensions as to the propriety of my being in the College when Matt clapped a hand on my shoulder and said, "Jim, the papers are making fun of this College as a useless thing. But believe me, I went through hell because of it. The anguish started last August at the Chicago convention. I came home heartsick at what our party had done to itself. And when they asked me to serve as an elector I wanted no part of it. But then I began to see that this could be a critical election. Wallace looked so strong that I thought he'd surely pick up enough votes to throw it into the House. And when the word got out that I was considering serving, men from all over, Republicans and Democrats alike, sought me out and said, 'Matt, you've got to accept. We don't know how this thing is going to end. And if the Electoral College becomes important, we want someone like you in there.' So I accepted, and then the sweating began, because I knew that if this fracas turned out to be inconclusive and threatened to go to the House, I was going to do everything in my power to bring the two major parties together to settle it in the Electoral College."

I asked, "Wouldn't that have been illegal?"

Matt said, "It would have been obligatory."

I asked, "How would you have started?"

Matt said, "I'd have started with you."

I asked, "What could we have accomplished?"

Matt said, "We could have destroyed any party that tried a corrupt deal. Because Republicans of like mind would have joined us."

I asked, "Do you think we could have won?"

Matt said, "It would have been a colossal brawl."

At this point I confided what my own plans had been, and like two conspirators we spent the hour prior to the opening of the College discussing how we had intended using that College for a commendable purpose. It became apparent as we talked that there would have been across the nation many like us, so concerned with the safety of our nation that we would have done whatever was legal to insure that safety. We were satisfied, each of us, that what we had proposed to ourselves was legal; and we were sure that it was necessary. We were struck by the fact that so far as we knew, no discussion of our intention had been conducted by any newspaper or television pundits. Pondering the matter each to himself, Gouger and I had stumbled upon this plan of action individually, yet our conclusions had been practically identical.

Nevertheless, we did feel as though we were plotters against the established good when we spotted the chairman of our Democratic party in Pennsylvania, Thomas Z. Minehart, coming over to greet us. He was an amiable man, a good lawyer, a good public servant who had been in state government for several decades and who had directed party battles for quite a few years. He was an ardent Democrat, having been tempered in the job of checking on Republican operations when that party held control of the state. He had seen his Democrats win and lose in their brawls with the Republicans, but had gained most of his scars as a result of intramural fights within his own party. He was canny, tough, big in body and gesture, as typical a state chairman as you could find. The best single way to characterize him, I suppose, would be to say that when Democrats lost, Tom Minehart bled. I judged that I had been chosen president of the College largely because Tom wanted me.

When the greetings were over he sighed and confessed, "I'll be very glad when this day is over."

I supposed he was speaking of the job he faced in lining up the eight substitute delegates. "Nine," he corrected. "One of the men from over the mountain just called in and said he couldn't make it."

"Did you find somebody?" I asked, for it was my duty to see that all ranks were filled.

"Yeah. We tagged Hugo Parente, the mayor of Monessen." He stopped, looked at us, and volunteered, "This day could have been a miserable one. If Wallace had won the number of votes he promised to win in September, this would have been one hell of a day."

"In what way?" Gouger asked in his Texas drawl, which seduces men into saying more than they had intended.

"I'll tell you what way," Minehart said. "You won't believe this, but if this election had been tied up in the Electoral College, I was prepared as state chairman of the Democratic party to assemble the leaders of our party and ask them to get together with the Republicans to strike a deal between us to settle this thing honorably, for the welfare of the nation. If our side had lost heavily in the popular vote, I would have had to go to men like you and Michener, supposing Pennsylvania had gone Democratic, and ask you to vote Republican."

It was Tom Minehart, the state chairman, as tough a Democrat as I have known, who was saying these words, and I asked him if I might write them down. He said, "Go ahead. We would have faced a national crisis, and at such a time we would all have had to act in strange new ways."

I asked him why he had reached this extraordinary conclusion, and he said, "Any party which would have made a deal with Wallace would have been destroyed for two generations. I don't want to see the Republican party destroyed, and God knows I don't want to see my own go down the drain."

At this point a secretary hurried up with the news that another of the delegates wasn't going to be able to make it, which meant that we were ten short. We had no more names of easily available Democrats, so we put in a few rush calls, with no success. The secretary said, "We've only a few minutes." She suggested one or two Democrats who might be staying at one of the Harrisburg hotels, but we couldn't locate them, so finally she said, "Mr. Minehart, you'll just have to be a delegate." It was agreed that Minehart would serve in this emergency although he would have preferred not to. "I'll be the tenth man," he said, and a Jewish bystander cracked, "Minehart the minyan," referring to the ancient synagogue rule that no religious service may be held therein without the presence of a minyan, or ten men, so that the latest arrival is hailed as he who makes the minyan.

As he left us Minehart said, "Of course, if the Democrats had been ahead in the popular vote, I'd have expected Bob Jordan to persuade his Republicans to make a deal with us. And I feel convinced the deal would have been made." I judged that what he was saying was that regardless of party there would have been enough electors of deep-seated conviction, of adherence to historical principles, to prevent the leaders of either major party from making a deal that would have been morally offensive. And it did not matter whether the electors were Republicans or Democrats. There would have been rebellion.

These somber thoughts were shattered by the booming of the most extraordinary voice in Pennsylvania politics. It was of piercing force, echoing throughout the whole area of the capitol where we stood. It was deep like a man's voice, but also penetrating like a woman's. We all turned, for it was familiar, and there, standing feebly with the aid of a cane, was a little old woman ninety-four years old, in a neat blue dress, with all her own teeth, and a raffish grin on her face.

"When we carried this state in 1936," the amazing voice boomed, "our party hadn't been in power for over fifty years and we didn't have one damned Democrat who knew a thing about procedures. Hell, we were like a bunch of country yokels."

It was Emma Guffey Miller, the grand old lady of our party and sister to the late Senator Joe Guffey. For years the two parties in Pennsylvania had grand women as their leaders, Mrs. Worthington Scranton for the Republicans and Mrs. Miller for the Democrats. The son of the first became governor of the state; the second watched her brother become the dominant senator. Mrs. Scranton had great wealth behind her, and she spent it well; Mrs. Miller had that incredible voice and the grandeur that comes of sheer persistence.

I first met her brother in the days when he was being elected as a Democrat from a state where his party did not particularly flourish. He therefore had to engage in a certain amount of showmanship, and this he did with aplomb. I remember one meeting in Quakertown, where some three hundred of us were waiting to hear him, and he had arranged for four young men in blue suits to appear at fifteen-minute intervals, all looking alike, all breathless with excitement as they rushed into the hall.

At nine that night the first young man in blue shouted, "Senator Guffey has just left Philadelphia!"

At nine-fifteen the second man cried breathlessly, "The Senator has just left Lansdale."

At nine-thirty the third man told us, "The Senator was seen in Sellersville."

And at nine forty-five the last young man gathered the other three about him and they all rushed into the room, bellowing, "Here he is now, Senator Guffey!"

Mrs. Miller was to be my vice-president and I thought I had better coach her as to what was involved, but she pushed me away grandly and announced, "Good God, young man! I was a member of this College back when Gifford Pinchot was governor. And I was a member three other times and I would have been three more times but the damned Republicans carried the state."

She looked extremely frail, so I asked her if when she presided over the election of the Vice-President of the United States, she would prefer a chair, and she bellowed, "Hell no. You stand me on that rostrum and I'll take care of things."

When I met with the other delegates I found that they had been the subject of a spirited mail campaign conducted by the so-called Commission on Election Reform, which sought to highlight the absurdities of a system whereby electors were free to vote for candidates whose names had not even appeared on the ballot. The commission, about which I could find nothing when I tried to call its headquarters in Seattle, Washington, was urging us to select as our next Vice-President a Seattle lawyer named Roderick D. Dimoff on the grounds that since he spoke Russian and French he could conduct international negotiations with Brezhnev and de Gaulle in their own languages. One delegate said, "If his reasons had been more persuasive we might have elected him." Because, of course, we were free to choose whomever we wished.

Later I discovered that the Commission on Election Reform was one man, Dimoff, and his campaign had attracted much attention in the west. Dimoff promised that in the unlikely event that he was chosen as Nixon's partner, "I would expect almost to be snubbed by him for thwarting his will. After that, I expect we probably could establish a relationship of cordial good will. I would work not to absorb any of his functions." He entered the race, he said, to draw attention to the fact that the electors could do whatever they wished. He made only one campaign promise: to go on a diet and lose sixty pounds so he wouldn't look so fat at government functions.

My attention was now distracted by a messenger who informed me that one of our substitute delegates, Roland Greenfield, was himself going to miss the opening gavel because the snowstorm had immobilized his car in Philadelphia. "I'm going to try to make it by train," he had told headquarters over the phone. We consulted as to what to do, and since we had no more substitutes on hand, we decided to start proceedings and trust that he would arrive before the time for swearing in of the delegates. My first half hour in command, therefore, was spent with one eye on the door to see whether we were indeed going to have twenty-nine electors.

When we opened with a prayer, Greenfield was absent. When we swore in the regularly elected electors, he was still missing. It was now time to swear in the substitute delegates and there was still no Greenfield. I held a whispered consultation as to what we should do, because no substitute elector is eligible to serve unless he has written authorization from the governor attesting to his credentials.

In the back of the room I saw the round and beaming face of Sam Frank of Allentown, and I whispered, "I'm sure Sam will serve if we need him."

We were about to conscript Sam, who I knew was a good Democrat, when the doors burst open and a very breathless Roland Greenfield arrived, just in time to be sworn in. By hook and by crook we had assembled twenty-nine duly authorized electors, and this same farce was being repeated today in all the fifty state capitols. These capriciously assembled men and women were free to determine history. One wondered why they had agreed to serve. Certainly it wasn't the pay—three dollars plus three cents a mile one way from their homes.

There was no uncertainty as to how the members felt about the College. Matt Gouger was telling everyone, "It ought to be abolished." Minehart told those seated near him, "It's served its usefulness." A committee working for reform asked for my signature to their petition and I gave it.

When Joe Kelley, secretary to the commonwealth and organizer of the College, spoke he said, "It may well be that the ancient drumbeat that brings us together better served a distant day. But so long as we do not choose to revise it, we will continue to march to the measure of its thought."

Governor Shafer was more blunt; he said, "However improbable, the constitutional fact is that you electors across the nation could upset the will of the American people as expressed last November 5, if you chose to disregard their mandate.

"The agony of those uncertain moments on election eve serve as sharp reminders that we must take positive action to safeguard our country against the specter of an undecided election. It is no reflection upon the grandeur of our Constitution to urge that we revise it in this area. The very generation that framed it moved swiftly to add the Twelfth Amendment in 1804 after the famous tie vote of the electors made impossible any choice between Burr and Jefferson.

"I will recommend that our General Assembly, when it convenes, lead the nation in a call to Congress for a constitutional amendment to abolish the Electoral College."

At this point an assistant whispered to me, "He's got guts. Telling us we're no good and asking us to go out of business. But he's right."

As president of the College, I was required to say a few words setting the stage for what we were about to do, and when I rose to speak, the farcical nature of the day was forgotten and its gravity became real indeed. I said, "In recent years I have worked in many foreign countries, and as I join with you here today to perform an important ritual, I think of my many friends abroad who would give much of what they own if only they could participate in a free election such as this, if only they could choose their leaders. As a member of the party that lost the election in November, I think it especially noteworthy that we can meet here under the protection of the majority party, with their governor to greet us amicably, with their employees to help us run our election. I have hundreds of friends abroad who would treasure the opportunity to contest an election, lose, and then be treated graciously by the victors. This is more remarkable than we might think."

I then explained briefly why there would be so much careful ritual of recorded votes and oaths and certifications and attested copies and repeated signatures. "In 1876 the states were not so careful. Their records were sloppy and inaccurate and in due time were challenged, so that for four months the nation did not know who its President was to be. Tilden had apparently won in both the popular and the electoral vote, but the records of Florida, Louisiana, Oregon, and South Carolina were contested, and finally all were thrown to Hayes, who won primarily because men like us had not done their job properly." We resolved that we would do ours in strict conformance to the law.

And then unfolded the pageantry of recording the vote six times, in most meticulous detail, so as to avoid a repetition of 1876. One of the six copies would go directly to the President of the Senate, two copies to the Secretary of the Commonwealth of Pennsylvania for filing, two copies to the Administrator of General Services in Washington. The sixth copy had an interesting significance:

RESOLVED, That one Elector of this College be appointed by the President to take in charge one of the packages containing one list of the Electors originally elected, one certificate of the election filling vacancies in the Electoral College, if any, and one certificate of the votes cast for the offices of President and Vice-President of the United States, and forward the same by Registered Mail through the Postmaster at the City of Harrisburg, Pennsylvania, to the Honorable Michael H. Sheridan, United States District Court, Scranton, Chief Judge of the District Court of the United States for the Middle District of Pennsylvania.

It had been found to be a good idea for one set of the records to be turned over to a judge who presumably could be trusted.

When the scratching of the pens had ended, when Emma Guffey Miller's powerful voice echoed across the gilded chamber, "When are we going to eat?" and when our work had been legally sealed into bundles for transmittal to the proper authorities, I banged the gavel and announced that Pennsylvania's Electoral College was adjourned, *sine die,* and as I left the rostrum I uttered a quiet prayer of thanks that this day had passed so uneventfully, when it could have been so destructive.

We had not yet left the capitol before a newsman advised us that in North Carolina the Republican elector, Dr. Lloyd W. Bailey, of Rocky Mount—who had said that he was proud of his membership in the right-wing John Birch Society—had arbitrarily refused to vote for Nixon and had voted for Wallace instead. Even without the pressures of an inconclusive election, one of the Nixon votes had defected; with the pressures that I have been describing, many more Republican votes would have vanished. The Democrats, too, suffered. In Michigan the former state chairman of the party, Zolton Ferency, refused as a matter of principle to cast his pledged vote for Humphrey; in this case he did not vote for someone else but resigned from the College so that a substitute chosen on the spot could vote for Humphrey. Again, the intense battles that I have been referring to had not developed, but already there was arbitrary action. Is any further proof needed for the condemnation of this system?

Furthermore, if the election had been thrown into the House, do you suppose for one moment that our Representatives, who are only electors made large, would have been immune to the extreme pressures that would have been generated, when one man's vote could determine the vote of an entire state, or perhaps the nation? There would have been a shambles beyond description. There was in the past and there would be in the future. Contemplating such an election in the House, a senior officer of that body said, "I hope to God I never see the day."

III

HOW
THE SYSTEM
GREW

IN CONTEMPLATING ELECTORAL REFORM AND IN TRYING TO DE-cide what pattern it should take, two definitions must be kept in mind. The United States functions under an electoral system, which has many good features; this system operates through an Electoral College, which has none. The definitions which I shall use follow:

Electoral system. A compromise plan worked out by the Founding Fathers in which the rights of large and small states are equally protected. It consists of five main features. (1) Election of the President shall not be by popular vote but by electoral. (2) Each state regardless of size shall have two electoral votes corresponding to its two senators, a protection to the small. (3) Each state shall also have one elector for each representative to which it is entitled in Congress, a protection to the large. (4) To be elected, a candidate must win a majority of the electoral vote. (5) Inconclusive elections are thrown into the House.

Electoral College. This phrase appears nowhere in the Constitution nor in any enabling legislation. It thus has no legal force and is merely a convenient mode of describing the electors when considered as a group. The exact meaning of the phrase is undetermined, for no one knows whether it signifies one of the fifty-one groups who assemble at each state capitol and the District of Columbia or the total body of 538 which never meets as a unit anywhere at any time. In popular usage, the phrase applies to the whole body of electors, who in normal elections serve only a ritual function; in emergencies, a vital one.

This essay argues that in the electoral system there is much worth salvaging; in the Electoral College, nothing. Therefore I shall pay most attention to the derivation of the former.

GENESIS OF THE ELECTORAL SYSTEM

When the Constitutional Convention assembled in Philadelphia in 1787, scant support was found for the election of the President by popular vote. (In this discussion I shall not mention the Vice-President. As Hugh Williamson of North Carolina explained in debate, "Such an officer as the Vice-President was not wanted. He was introduced only for the sake of a valuable mode of election which required two be chosen at the same time.")

The chief proponent of a popular vote was James Wilson of Pennsylvania, who argued that the President, the Senate, and the House should be elected by direct vote of the people so as to make them as independent as possible of each other. He was supported by Gouverneur Morris, also of Pennsylvania, who uttered the classic phrase, "If the President is to be the guardian of the people, let him be appointed by the people." James Madison of Virginia gave his grudging assent, pointing out that all proposed systems had defects but this seemed the best, since the President was to act for the people, and not the states.

Opponents of a direct popular vote were relentless in their attack on the plan, pointing out the defects which made it suspect in that age. Elbridge Gerry of Massachusetts, who in the end would refuse to sign the completed Constitution and would campaign against its ratification because it did not square with his ideas of theoretical republicanism nor provide sufficient safeguards against democracy, argued, "The people are uninformed and would be misled by a few designing men." Popular voting, he said, was radically vicious.

When the convention finally voted on the plan, the count was 2 to 9 against, with only Pennsylvania and Delaware in favor.

The proposal that elicited most support was one calling for Congress to elect the President. So many delegates and states considered this the only practical plan that it was generally supposed to prevail, and in four separate votes it did; it also appeared in the provisional draft of final recommendations and was about as close to being finally adopted as a proposal could have been without becoming an official part of the Constitution.

Reasons adduced in favor were obvious: most of the states chose their governors by this system; the Congress, being "the depository of the supreme will of the society," ought naturally to appoint the executive, who would then be accountable to it; and the dangers of a popular vote of the people would be avoided.

Why did a plan so popular and so logical at that time finally fail when at one vote it passed unanimously, at another, 8 to 2, and again 7 to 4? It seems in retrospect that protracted debate, and especially the attacks by Gouverneur Morris and James Wilson, laid bare every weakness until in the end all saw that a President chosen by the Congress would perforce have to become subservient to Congress. One by one the defenders of such election drifted away and in the end a Committee of Eleven was appointed to arrange a compromise, but a last-ditch effort was made to force Congressional election onto the convention. This time it failed 2 to 8 and the concept was dead.

The Committee of Eleven was an able group representing all shades of political opinion in the convention, and it worked four days without interruption seeking a solution to the impasse. It decided early not to return either to direct popular election or to choice by Congress. The alternative that was finally chosen seems to have been voiced first by James Wilson, who had concluded, when his plan of direct voting was defeated, that intermediary electors might be the solution. At any rate, the committee reported to the floor the plan under which we operate today. The compromise was five-fold, as outlined earlier: electoral vote, not popular; two votes for senators; one for each representative; winner must have a majority; inconclusive elections to the House.

It was a brilliant compromise; not only was it the solution to the convention impasse, later it would also aid conspicuously in obtaining from the states the ratification votes necessary to put the Constitution into operation. It was thus the rock of decision, the keystone without which all else would have been impossible, and it is enshrined in the success our nation has had in the difficult task of keeping a federal union of equals together and functioning. Technically the plan had many faults, as we shall see; philosophically it was impeccable.

In the public discussion of the proposed Constitution, and in the *Federalist Papers* which played so strong a role in winning support, there was surprisingly little discussion of the compromise method for electing a President. The Founding Fathers were well satisfied with themselves and felt that they had produced a system which would last indefinitely. It is true that in the final debates within the convention itself Madison had warned that election in the House carried certain built-in pitfalls, but corrections had been made to accommodate his sharpest criticisms and he did not publicly repeat his attack. Hamilton confidently assured the public, "The mode of appointment of the chief magistrate of the United States is almost the only part of the system, of any consequence, which has escaped without severe censure, or which has received the slightest mark of approbation from its opponents."

I am surprised that this group of keen politicians and social philosophers should have failed to anticipate the two rocks on which their plan would founder. First, they did not foresee the rise of political parties or the way in which they would destroy the effectiveness of the electors. Second, they did not guess that election by the House would work so poorly. This blindness on the part of the best leadership this nation has ever produced should give one pause if he thinks that in the next few years our current leadership will be able to come up with corrections that will end past abuses without introducing new. There could well be unforeseen weaknesses in our plans that would produce results just as unexpected as those which overtook the first great plan.

DEVELOPMENT OF THE SYSTEM

If one looks at our first three Presidential elections, one might conclude that the electoral plan had worked as proposed. In 1789 the electors did meet in their own states, they did consider the great men of our nation, and they did settle upon George Washington, by a vote of 69 to 0. In 1792 they did the same, by a vote of 132 to 0. In 1796, when for the first time there was a real contest, the system still proved effective, for the electors met, studied the credentials of the grand figures still among them, and chose John Adams over Thomas Jefferson, by a vote of 71 to 68. It is true that factionalism and not philosophy dictated the choice between the two men, and it is also true that the debacle of 1800 was ominously presaged when certain leaders in Adams' party entered into a cabal to give Thomas Pinckney of South Carolina the same number of votes as Adams, with the idea of making Pinckney President when the election went to the House. This was forestalled by the fact that Jefferson slipped into second position, thus eliminating Pinckney, but this produced its own unacceptable result: President Adams and Vice-President Jefferson were of different factions and not personally congenial.

The 1800 election magnified these weaknesses and proved certain aspects of the system were not only ineffective but also corrupting. Whereas Pinckney supporters in 1796 had lost in their gamble of forcing a tie vote which could have been used to deny Adams the Presidency, in 1800 Burr had engineered just such a vote and had nearly succeeded in this disreputable stratagem. Furthermore, when the brutal battle was over, Jefferson wound up with Burr as his Vice-President, a pairing that must have been intolerable to both men.

The principal reason the original electoral plan was producing so many unexpected results was that early in the life of our republic political parties emerged with an importance no one had foreseen, and electors quickly saw that if they consolidated their vote behind their party's choice, they would gain a considerable advantage, and this they did. The splendid original concept of men of high principle convening to pass upon the credentials of those who might lead the nation had swiftly degenerated into the practical maneuver of party hacks meeting to confirm the choice their party had already made. As early as 1800 every elector but one cast a straight party vote.

The fact that a noble concept should have failed was not exceptional; the fact that the failure was not corrected was. The Twelfth Amendment did eliminate the chance of another Adams-Pinckney or Jefferson-Burr misunderstanding as to who was running for what, but it continued the office of elector—already discredited—and made no significant changes in the procedure by which the House voted for President, although it did allow a choice to be made from the three top candidates instead of two, as before.

Starting in 1796 three parallel lines of accidental development determined the character of our election system, and not one was a result of either constitutional amendment or Congressional law. The vital processes I now speak of were the result of custom. When occasionally they were reinforced by state law, the statutes were of the most diverse nature.

Election of the electors. Both the Constitution and the Twelfth Amendment leave the method of selecting electors to the judgment of the various states, and we have seen how varied that can be. At the start most states gave their legislatures the job of designating electors, but custom forced the rapid decline of this tradition. In 1800 ten states out of sixteen used that method; in 1824, six out of twenty-four; and by 1832 the practice had practically vanished, only South Carolina clinging to this concept through the election of 1860. (When Colorado was admitted to the union in 1876 she allowed her legislature to pick her electors, as did Florida in that same year, but these were curiosities to be quickly abandoned.) Custom had dictated a significant change in the system.

Observe that insofar as the Constitution is concerned, any state is free to distribute its electors among the various parties as it wishes; in the early elections, if a given state wanted to split its electoral vote between Federalists and Republican-Democrats it was free to do so, and many did. For example, in 1800 the Pennsylvania legislature designated eight electors for Jefferson and seven for Adams. As we shall see shortly, the concept that all of a state's electoral votes must go to the candidate who wins a bare plurality of the popular vote is a later innovation without constitutional sponsorship.

Also, in the early years those few states which did elect their electors often used the district plan, rather than choosing the entire ticket at large. Of the five states that elected in 1800, two did so at large, three by district; in 1824 it was twelve at large, five by district; and in 1836, twenty-five at large, none by district. However, as late as 1892 the Democrats in Michigan, tired of seeing that state's 14 electoral votes go automatically to the Republicans, forced through a measure which provided for district election, which produced the results they sought, Republicans 9 to Democrats 5; but the state quickly saw that by thus splitting its vote it was putting itself at a disadvantage compared to states which did not, and the experiment ended.

Electors bound to vote as their state voted. The custom developed in the late years of the eighteenth century, was ironbound by 1804 and has been recognized in various state laws, as we saw in the opening chapter. At this date, in only sixteen states and the District of Columbia does election law make it clear that the elector is expected to vote as his state voted. To cite only two such laws: *Connecticut General Statutes,* 1967 revision: "Each such elector shall cast his ballots for the candidates under whose name he ran on the official election ballot." *Nevada Revised Statutes,* 1965: "The Presidential electors shall vote only for the nominees for President and Vice-President of the party that prevailed in this State in the preceding general election." The nebulous value of such law has been demonstrated earlier.

Winner-take-all distribution of electoral votes. This is the most radical development within our electoral system and one that the framers of the Constitution seem not to have anticipated. Although there was much stated fear of domination by large states, the delegates did not foresee by what a relatively simple tactic this was to come about. Originally it was intended that the prudent electors of a state with five votes might divide 3 to 2 or even 2–2–1. When the votes of these separate delegations—who were not allowed to meet in union—were counted in Congress some months later, the name of the next President would be known.

It did not take long for a large state to see that if it prevailed upon its electors to vote as a bloc, its leverage would be consolidated and magnified, which would be especially important if one of the candidates happened to be a resident of that state. Once one state made this discovery and acted upon it, all had to follow. By 1800 this principle was widely recognized; in 1804, of the ten states that chose electors by popular vote, seven allotted all their electors to the party that had won the election; in 1824 thirteen out of eighteen did so, and by 1836 it was a nationwide custom with few exceptions.

By 1836, therefore, the principal features of our haphazard system were determined and no changes have since occurred in the areas we have been discussing. Such amendments as we have had since the major revision provided by the Twelfth Amendment in 1804 have concerned other matters that required attention. The Seventeenth in 1913 stipulated the popular election of United States senators. The Nineteenth in 1920 gave the vote to women. The Twentieth in 1933 related to the terms of President and Vice-President and the convening of the incoming Congress. The Twenty-second in 1951 limited a President to two full terms. The Twenty-third in 1961 gave the District of Columbia electoral votes. The Twenty-fourth in 1964 barred poll taxes in federal elections. And the Twenty-fifth in 1967 clarified the question of Presidential succession and disability. But the fundamental electoral system was not affected by any of these. It is true that from time to time Congressional statute has clarified certain difficult technical points, and to see how this has occurred, let us look briefly at one election which produced reform.

THE STOLEN ELECTION

The chief characteristic of our system of electing a President has been pragmatism. When the Constitutional Convention first assembled, not a delegate, so far as we can now ascertain, was in favor of the plan that was finally adopted; it is possible that none had even considered it seriously, but out of pragmatic compromise it was born. Furthermore, most of its basic components were also compromises within the original. To take one example: as drafted, the basic compromise sent deadlocked elections to the Senate, but belatedly it was pointed out that to give this branch of Congress the right not only to confirm Presidential appointments but also to elect in the first place was to make the President a creature of the Senate. Even so, when doughty James Wilson proposed that right of election be moved to the House, he was defeated by a vote of 3 to 7. Next day Wilson was back with the observation that the plan as it then stood meant that "the President will not be the man of the people as he ought to be, but the minion of the Senate." This time Wilson lost 4 to 6. How was the matter resolved? By a secondary compromise. Roger Sherman of Connecticut and Hugh Williamson of North Carolina proposed that the election go to the House, but that there each state would have but one vote. This pragmatic solution passed 10 to 1.

I am always refreshed when I read of the common-sense role played by James Wilson; of all the delegates he seems best to have anticipated the temper of the future. A fierce proponent of the rights of the people, an adversary to all that would vest government in the hands of a few, he suffered more defeats of his individual proposals than almost any other delegate, yet in the end his larger ideas prevailed. After his work at the convention, he helped write Pennsylvania's second constitution, served in Congress and on the federal Supreme Court, where he delivered several pace-setting opinions. He was a Scotsman, a graduate of St. Andrews University, and in the years when I attended that school, the students conducted an annual pageant in which the great men who had studied there in past centuries paraded in antique costume to inspect and advise the contemporary students. As an American, I was always given the job of impersonating Wilson, and thus was driven to discover something about the man whose body, dress, and manner I was assuming, and the more I found out, the more impressed I became with the solid pragmatism he had carried from Scotland to Pennsylvania.

I would suppose, therefore, that the genius of our election system has best been expressed when the nation has faced an election crisis, discovered an inadequacy, and moved swiftly to correct it. I think no man could successfully argue that the compromise devised by the convention was totally good; the defects were too many and too grave, the invitation to fraud too enticing. But at numerous climaxes the nation has patched the system, or allowed custom slowly to evolve new forms that have sufficed; and the advantage of the whole has been that it has worked. The stubborn pragmatism of James Wilson and his colleagues has allowed us to elect a series of reasonably good Presidents in reasonable calm. But where troubles have arisen they have been corrected, and if we now do nothing in the face of the troubles I have been discussing, we shall be false to the spirit of our system. From time to time it needs patching; we are delinquent in our historical duty if we fail to apply the patches.

Nothing could better illustrate this principle than the election of 1876. The Republican candidate was a large, amiable Cincinnati lawyer whose outward aplomb reminds one of a later President from the same state, Warren G. Harding, but whose performance when elected was much superior. A law graduate from Harvard, with a modest hankering for politics and a flair for catching and holding public approbation, he was in the Union army in July, 1864, when leaders of his district proposed that he run for Congress. From his encampment he wrote: "An officer fit for duty who at this crisis would abandon his post to electioneer for a seat in Congress ought to be scalped." This statement, widely broadcast, ensured his election, whereupon he promptly resigned his commission, went to Washington, and served in the House of Representatives from 1865 to 1867.

After having served twice as governor of Ohio, he was denied a third term and returned to the law, but when a vacancy on the Republican gubernatorial ticket opened up in 1875, he was approached by the leaders of his party and asked to run again. In his diary he wrote: "Several suggest that if elected governor now, I will stand well for the Presidency next year. How wild! What a queer lot we are becoming."

In the Republican Convention in 1876 he had little chance of winning the nomination, for a group of able men stood ahead of him, but as in the Harding case there was a deadlock, and after six unproductive ballots he was put forward as the compromise candidate. Handsome, polished, well spoken, and gifted in recalling if not waving "the bloody shirt" of southern rebellion, Rutherford B. Hayes was a formidable candidate, exactly the kind required to gloss over the scandals that were erupting across the face of the Grant administration.

His Democratic opponent was Samuel J. Tilden, a strange man, moody, a retiring bachelor, a patrician railroad lawyer who had invested his substantial fees to build a personal fortune of more than $6,000,000 and who had built a strong reputation as a reformer by sending members of the Tweed ring to jail. On a strong reform platform he had become governor of New York. If Hayes reminds one of Harding, Tilden is clearly suggestive of Adlai Stevenson.

The Democrats had a good chance of winning this election, for by capturing the House in 1874 they had won a platform from which they could attack Grant and his corrupt administration. The scandals their investigating committees uncovered provided powerful campaign material and in the hands of a more vibrant popular leader would have swept the nation. As it was, Tilden's reticent campaign produced a popular majority of 251,746 and an electoral vote of 204 to 165, with only 185 needed to win.

But even before the Democrats could celebrate, Republican managers circulated reports that because of faulty or duplicate certification, the electoral votes of four states were in question, and these four states provided an interesting total of votes: Florida 4, Louisiana 8, South Carolina 7, Oregon 1. (Oregon had three votes, but the other two had been cast for Hayes without protest.) If these twenty contested votes were subtracted from the Tilden column and added to the Hayes, the result would be Hayes 185 to Tilden 184. The problem for the Republicans therefore became how to swing those contested votes into the Hayes column? Observe that it would do the Republicans no good if they won 19 of the votes; they had to win all 20, and their chances of doing so were extremely remote. But they set about the task.

What were the facts? Each of the four states had submitted to Congress two sets of returns. Those of the three southern states were drastically contradictory, one set giving all of that state's votes to Tilden, the other all to Hayes. In Oregon, however, the first set gave Hayes a count of 3 to 0, while the second gave him only 2 to 1. A fact of signal importance was that the Hayes votes from Louisiana had been obtained by the fraudulent device of having a Republican election board in one district reject several thousand Democratic ballots. In the Louisiana case at least, Tilden's chances looked ironclad, and in the Florida and South Carolina, good. It seemed certain that he must be the next President.

The Oregon case could go either way. The contested Hayes vote there had been cast by an elector who had forgotten to disclose that he was a postmaster, hence a federal employee, hence ineligible to serve. The Democratic governor took it upon himself to disbar this postmaster and to certify in his stead the Democratic elector with the highest number of votes, to which the Republicans countered by having the postmaster resign, which made him eligible, and submitting their own list of electors with his name on it. At this point the reader should determine how he would have treated that Oregon vote had he been on the commission reviewing the matter, because if the Florida, South Carolina, and Louisiana votes were all given to Hayes, the outcome of the election would hinge on this single vote.

Who was to adjudicate this ticklish question? On this point the Constitution was beautifully vague; it began clearly enough; it said that when the results of the electoral vote in each state had been submitted to the president of the Senate, that official should "in the Presence of the Senate and House of Representatives, open all the Certificates, and the Votes shall then be counted." Grammatically, if the framers had intended the president of the Senate to do the counting—and therefore the accepting and accrediting—their sentence would have read "The President of the Senate shall open all the Certificates and count them." By phrasing the instructions as they did, they apparently meant that the Congress itself should do the validating and counting.

The vital questions were phrased thus: Did the president of the

Senate count the votes, the Congress being mere witnesses; or did the Congress count them, the president's duty being merely to preside? And was the counting process merely mechanical or did it also entail validation of the reports as legal? A further question was not asked at that time, but it haunted the proceedings: What should be done in such a situation if the Senate were Republican and the House Democratic, as they were in 1877?

I suppose one could argue that the framers ought to have anticipated a situation like this, but they did not, so once again pragmatic solutions were called for. It should surprise no one that Congress decided it had the right to count and to accept or reject, but with the two houses in opposite hands politically, how precisely was Congress to perform these two functions? A compromise was reached whereby an electoral commission was established to which the Senate would appoint three of its Republican members and two Democrats; the House, three Democrats and two Republicans; and to which would be added two Republican Supreme Court justices, two Democratic, plus a fifth to be chosen by those four. Obviously, since the Republicans and Democrats could be expected to vote their party interests down the line, this fifth judge would determine the election.

The commission contained names famous in American history: from the Senate, the Republicans Edmunds of Vermont, Morton of Indiana, Frelinghuysen of New Jersey, and the Democrats Thurman of Ohio and Bayard of Delaware; from the House, the Democrats Payne of Ohio, Hunton of Virginia, Abbott of Massachusetts, and the Republicans Hoar of Massachusetts, Garfield of Ohio. Of this group, Frelinghuysen would become a Secretary of State, and Hoar would be famed in Congressional history; Morton would be a serious candidate for the Presidential nomination, and Garfield would achieve the Presidency. But in certain respects it was Bayard of Delaware who best epitomized American history, for his grandfather had been in the House during the Jefferson-Burr impasse in 1801 and had been the middleman who had arranged the final disposition of that deadlock. He had solved it by convincing Vermont and Maryland backers of Burr that they should refrain from voting, a policy which he himself followed.

The Democratic House had agreed to submit Tilden's fortunes to this commission on the understanding that the fifth judge would be Justice David Davis, born in Maryland but now a resident of Illinois, ostensibly a Republican but with a high-handed tendency toward independent action. Davis was a man of gargantuan size; it was said that when he needed new trousers he went not to the tailor but to the surveyor. As a rural lawyer he had early formed the habit of buying up any real estate that was sold at distress for taxes or mortgages, and on a modest salary, had accumulated a fortune of more than $2,000,000. It is true that Lincoln had appointed him to the Supreme Court as a Republican, but judging from his behavior in later years, he would have been impartial, mercurial, arbitrary, and self-directed in his decisions on the 20 contested votes, and it is inconceivable that he would have voted consistently one way or the other. With David Davis as the crucial fifteenth member of the commission, Tilden's election was assured.

And then an incomprehensible thing happened. The fact that the 20 votes would be contested had been determined on December 6, 1876. The bill authorizing the compromise commission was passed on January 26, 1877. This would have paved the way for the Democrats to maneuver the nomination of Davis as the fifteenth member; but just the afternoon before, the Democrats of Illinois, to settle a petty problem confronting them, had reached out to the Supreme Court of the United States and elected Justice David Davis to be their junior senator from Illinois. The Democratic plan had been torpedoed by thoughtless Democrats; the fifteenth man would now have to be some other judge; and what he would do on the commission no one could predict.

To follow Davis for a moment, he entered a Senate that was evenly balanced between Republicans and Democrats, and on numerous bills he constituted the balance of power. By deep conviction a Republican, by his experience on the Supreme Court a liberal Democrat, he vacillated on every vote until it was said of him that he had jumped from the bench to the fence; in his later years he voted mainly Republican, thus incurring the enmity of the Illinois Democrats who had given him his position at such a heavy cost to their party. It does seem likely that had he been the fifteenth man he would have split his vote and elected Tilden.

With his departure the four Supreme Court judges already appointed to the commission had to find another of their number, and they settled finally on Associate Justice Joseph P. Bradley, the only man in our history who could accurately claim that he alone had determined who was to be President of the Union. Born in New York State and educated at Rutgers, he was a fastidious man who bore little in common with the giant Davis. He was a corporation lawyer, but also a first-class accountant who had deduced the rules for the perpetual calendar that one finds in almanacs giving the day of the week for any date since the birth of Christ and on to infinity. He worked for one of America's largest insurance companies, but had as his hobby the genealogy of his family, which he compiled in exhaustive detail. When this was completed in several volumes he turned to his wife's family, and then to various branches and collateral connections.

He had once run for Congress on the Republican ticket, had served as head of New Jersey's electoral delegation when that state went for the Republican Grant in 1868, and had been appointed to the Supreme Court by a grateful Grant under circumstances that seemed dubious at the time and have not seemed less so with the passage of years. Almost immediately upon his appointment he led the Court in reversing a decision which had angered the Republican leadership.

On the surface, therefore, Bradley was a self-admitted Republican, but in his six years on the bench he had shown a marked individuality, and some of his later decisions had given the outward appearance of at least considering the Democratic point of view, so the commission accepted him, largely because there was no alternative. From the moment he took his place on the commission he voted straight Republican.

When there were indications that he was going to do so, throwing the election to Hayes, the Democrats began to show anxiety. They realized that the Florida, South Carolina, and Oregon decisions would probably go against them, but they trusted that the arrogant fraud in Louisiana would prove so malodorous that even Justice Bradley would have to vote with them. This became the central issue of the contest and it was debated on a high intellectual level. Democrats argued that the commission had not only the right but also the obligation to go behind the formal ballots and inquire into the basic truths of the matter; Republicans argued that Congress had no authority for questioning the integrity of a state. On this point, as on all others, Justice Bradley sided with the Republicans; with an undeviating vote of 8 to 7, every contest was settled in favor of Hayes, and on March 2, two days before inauguration, he was declared the winner, 185 to 184. On Saturday night, March 3, Hayes took the Presidential oath in a private White House ceremony, repeating the pledge in public on Monday, March 5.

Most accounts of this protracted battle, which brought our nation to the fracture point, overlook an extraordinary aspect of the case: the Democratic House, burning with resentment over the way it had been defrauded, met in separate session on March 3 and officially declared that Tilden had been elected President, thus nullifying the actions of the combined Congress. Since the Constitution clearly stated that in deadlocked elections the House shall choose, this was an open invitation to Democrats across the nation to reject Hayes; but by the miracle which seems to preserve us in these matters, the nation did just the opposite. It accepted the decision, and Hayes, who proved a flabby man, took the Presidency from Tilden, who then and always was a man of character and strength. Accepting his defeat he said graciously, "I can return to private life with the consciousness that I shall receive from posterity the credit of having been elected to the highest position in the gift of the people without any of the cares and responsibilities of the office." His lasting memorial is the New York Public Library, of which the Tilden Library, endowed by him, became an important part.

In 1887 the problems that had agitated the nation in 1876 were pragmatically settled, for Congress passed an election law which laid down procedures to be followed whenever the reports of the states to Congress were challenged in that body. In most important details the new law sustained the arguments which the Republicans had advanced in 1877. Congress was given the right to accept or reject state reports if they evidenced technical faults but was denied the right to look behind the integrity of a state's report. Furthermore, to avoid the possibility of another fifteen-man commission to determine validity, the new law said that if upon presentation to the joint session of Congress, a state's report is challenged by a member of each house, the two houses shall immediately convene separately and vote upon the matter. If both houses agree to accept or reject, that decision is final. "But if the two Houses [acting separately] shall disagree in respect of the counting of such votes, then, and in that case, the votes of the electors whose appointment shall have been certified by the executive of the State, under the seal thereof, shall be counted."

Had I been one of the Democratic commissioners in the 1877 contest, the Louisiana problem would have posed a dilemma, for I would have agreed with the Republicans that Congress had no right to go behind a state's declaration, but I would also have known that unless Congress did, we Democrats would lose. I remembered this when Republicans in 1960 were crying for a Congressional investigation into the Illinois vote; what Illinois reported those votes to be established the fact, and if fraud had been committed, its correction lay not in Congress but in Illinois.

One aspect of this haphazard election was to bear unexpected consequences. When Democrats in the House threatened to take action which would nullify the impending theft of the Presidency, a deal was proposed to silence them. If the southern Democrats would look the other way, Hayes would pledge that when elected he would end Reconstruction governments in South Carolina and Louisiana and withdraw federal occupation troops from all parts of the south. This was a sensible compromise in that the most pressing problem before the incoming President, whoever he might be, was the reconciliation of the Union, and of the two contenders, Hayes was best suited to accomplish this. The deal was struck, the bargain kept. Hayes got the Presidency. The south got back its governments. But what Hayes did not anticipate was that those governments quickly became lily-white; the principles of the Ku Klux Klan were allowed to dominate; the south became solidly Democratic; and the interminable suppression of the Negro was revived. It would be too much to claim that this was the result of a faulty election system, but it does reflect the kind of deal men are forced into when the system is inexact and vulnerable to negotiation.

Equally germane to our present discussion is the timetable of the 1876 crisis. Constitutional questions arising from it were not settled satisfactorily until 1887, a delay of eleven years, in spite of the fact that correction involved mere law and not a constitutional amendment. At the end of this essay, when I speculate as to how rapidly we might correct the flaws made evident in 1968, this long delay will be a precedent; but so will the earlier crisis of 1800. The flaw uncovered in that election was so flagrant that corrective action of drastic dimension was completed within three and one half years (final vote on Jefferson-Burr, February 17, 1801; submission of a proposed amendment to the states, December 8, 1803; ratification by three fourths of the states, July 27, 1804; amendment effective, September 25, 1804, in time to govern the Presidential election held that November). This too is a precedent to keep in mind.

TWO BIZARRE PROPOSALS

Because the American people have got to face up to the reckless gamble they are taking with the Presidency, it is necessary now to explore two proposals that were made only semi-seriously during the 1968 campaign but which deserve serious consideration, since each was practical and in the future might tempt desperate men who want to grab the Presidency.

When it became apparent that Wallace was going to siphon off a respectable number of electoral votes and perhaps prevent either Nixon or Humphrey from winning, it was proposed in various quarters that two alternative courses of action could make Nelson Rockefeller President. In the first case, suppose the division of votes to have been Nixon 248, Humphrey 248, Wallace 42, which would produce not only an inconclusive electoral vote but also a fairly balanced distribution of state delegations in the House, so that neither Nixon nor Humphrey could have counted upon a victory there, either.

In this impasse a beautiful stratagem lay open to the Rockefeller forces: simply persuade the New York electoral delegation of 43 votes to cast them for Rockefeller, who would then wind up in third place in the electoral voting, one vote ahead of Wallace, and would be one of the three names sent to the House, the other two being Nixon and Humphrey, neither of whom had a probability of victory. Then, in the House, a deal could be struck between the deadlocked Republicans and Democrats whereby Rockefeller, who might prove acceptable to both, would be given the Presidency upon his pledge to conduct a bipartisan administration.

In the second instance, imagine the vote to have been Nixon 234, Humphrey 234, Wallace 70, with an evenly divided House. New York's electoral votes alone will not project Rockefeller into third place, but all that is required is for Pennsylvania to join the compact, and with her votes Rockefeller again winds up in third position, with two votes more than Wallace, and is again put forth to the House as a compromise candidate satisfactory to both parties.

This is not preposterous. New York and Pennsylvania laws do not punish electors of their states for voting as they wish; they are not constitutionally bound by election results, and if they preferred Rockefeller to the alternatives, they could have voted for him, with the results as indicated. There may be readers who would have preferred Rockefeller to either of the two major candidates, but no man should be elevated to the Presidency by a trick of this nature. The simple way to protect ourselves is to revise our election laws.

The second strange proposal preoccupied me from the moment I thought of becoming an elector, and I am surprised that not more critics of our system have been aware of its possibility. Article II of the Constitution first enunciated a principle which has never been altered. It consists of two clearly worded statements: The electors "shall make a List of all the Persons voted for . . . and transmit sealed . . . to the President of the Senate." If the vote is inconclusive, "then the House of Representatives shall immediately choose by ballot." In the Twelfth Amendment the two words *immediately choose* were reversed as a matter of style, but the basic law remained the same.

The question is: to which Congress does the list of electoral votes go, the old one or the new? And which House is entitled to do the choosing? Prior to the election I showed this provision to the fifty men and women of whom I spoke earlier and asked them what the words meant. Half said, "Of course it means the Congress in being now"—that is, the 90th; the other half said with equal conviction, "Naturally it means the incoming Congress"—that is, the 91st. The question has never been adjudicated; only custom, written into law in 1934, has determined that it should be the incoming Congress which receives the electoral count and the incoming House that elects the President in case of deadlock. Any Congress has full authority to change that law.

In this ambiguity, suppose that in the November, 1968, election the results had been inconclusive and, furthermore, that the House had switched from the Democratic majority in the 90th Congress to a Republican majority in the 91st. It would have been simple and legal for a disgruntled President Johnson, as soon as he saw what the alignments were, to summon a special session of the old Democratic Congress for the purpose of revoking the law of 1934 and establishing an earlier date for counting the electoral vote. By this simple device the votes of the Electoral College would have been delivered to the lame-duck Congress and certified by it, whereupon the Democratic House could have proceeded to "choose immediately" Hubert Humphrey as President.

I grant that it would have been unwise for President Johnson to attempt this; I grant that it would have been a cynical attack upon our system thus to force upon us a President we might not have

wanted; and I grant that Republicans in the Senate might have fili-
bustered throughout December to repel the circumvention. But I
also grant that under our present laws the effort would have been
legal. I can easily foresee emergency situations in which this tactic
could be used against the general welfare and the wishes of the people. It can easily be forestalled by a simple declaration in the next
amendment as to which Congress has the authority.

The point that must be stressed in any evaluation of our present
system is that it is founded partly on the Constitution, mainly on in-
herited custom. There is no reason why we should not change the
latter if it no longer serves us; nor is there any reason why we should
not change the constitutional framework too, if it is proving faulty. I
think we misuse patriotism if we fall back upon it as a reason for re-
jecting change in our Constitution, and I thank Neal R. Peirce for
citing in his excellent book *The People's President,* James Madison's
confession on the matter we are discussing: "The difficulty of finding
an unexceptionable process for appointing the Executive Organ of a
Government such as that of the U.S., was deeply felt by the Convention; and as the final arrangement took place in the latter stages of
the session, it was not exempt from a degree of the hurrying influence
produced by fatigue and impatience in all such bodies; tho' the degree was much less than usually prevails in them."[*] The convention
was nodding when it approved some of the provisions in the great
compromise, and they should be corrected.

---

[*]Many subjects dealt with in this essay are developed in much greater detail in
Peirce's *The People's President* (New York, Simon and Schuster, 1968), which reaches
certain conclusions contrary to mine.

IV

CERTAIN
SENSIBLE
PROPOSALS

I T MUST BE APPARENT TO ANY SERIOUS STUDENT OF OUR POLITI-
cal system, and to even the most casual voter who has the best interests of his nation at heart, that we ought to take steps immediately
to abolish both the Electoral College and the choosing of Presidents
by the House of Representatives. On these two points there appears
to be unanimity, but as to what we should do after these corrections
have been made, there is considerable difference of honest opinion,
and I should now like to explore both the proposals and the opinions,
masking, if I can, my own preferences, which will be stated later.

But before I proceed I must put forth certain fundamental principles which underlie anything I have to say about government, for
these convictions, gathered for the most part from the writings and
experiences of our Founding Fathers, have served me as guidelines
through all my thinking on politics, both in this nation and in the
others in which I have worked.

I apologize for the intrusion of certain personal references. I write
not as an author of books; I write as one who has been deeply concerned about the government of this nation and of all nations. In
1960 I served as a county chairman for Senator John F. Kennedy and
campaigned for him across the country. In 1962 I ran for Congress in
Bucks and Lehigh Counties in Pennsylvania, and lost, in part be-

cause I was up against a long-term incumbent who knew precisely what was required to hold onto his seat in his district, and in part because my opponent had a registration superiority of about 20,000 votes, which is a good thing to have in an election. In 1964 I campaigned on behalf of President Lyndon B. Johnson in three states, and in 1968 I not only worked vigorously for Vice-President Hubert H. Humphrey in a frantic airplane caravan but also wrote his official campaign biography.

In 1967 I served as secretary to the Pennsylvania Constitutional Convention and helped engineer a revision which would bring Pennsylvania into the forefront of states insofar as a modernized, constructive constitution was concerned. In this enterprise I had the opportunity of working at close quarters with William Scranton, former governor, who provided our convention with the moral stability and leadership any such group requires; it was partly because of Scranton that Pennsylvania became the only recent state to achieve a complete reform of its constitution, New York, Maryland, Rhode Island, and others having tried and failed. I speak favorably of Scranton because when the time came for the voters of our state to accept or reject the new constitution, Chief Justice John Bell, of our Supreme Court, and his associate, Justice Michael Musmanno, leveled blasts against it of such weight and fury that it would have been defeated had not Scranton addressed the people of the state in these measured terms: "The charges made against the proposed changes by Justices Bell and Musmanno are the charges of two distinguished, nit-picking elderly statesmen who are interested not in the welfare of the state but in their personal prerogatives. If you voters decide to throw out the splendid work we have done for you, the best revision I am sure that this state could have produced, then you are out of your minds." I cite these extraordinary words because I believe they could serve as copy-texts in the months ahead when proposals to change our system of electing Presidents are brought before the people for their acceptance or rejection.

Finally, in 1968 I served as co-chairman of a special committee charged with submitting recommendations for the general overhaul of procedures by which the Pennsylvania legislature operates. I would hope that in the years ahead I would continue to find the energy to work in politics, for I consider it one of the most fruitful exercises of the human mind.

The following are the three basic principles which have governed my attitude toward the mechanics of government, it being assumed that other principles of similar weight—such as justice, equality, economic stability, and a judicious respect for historical derivations—determined my attitude toward the moral aspects of government.

Legitimacy. The more I see of nations and the manner in which they govern themselves the more convinced I become that a prime requirement of any good government is that it be legitimate, that its sources of power be clear-cut and aboveboard, that its citizens accept decisions as honestly derived. People must see for themselves that laws are honestly passed, that Supreme Court decisions are untainted, that Presidents are fairly chosen.

In ancient days it was a priestly prerogative and obligation to bear public witness to the fact that kings descended legitimately one from the other, and great effort was spent to trace out lineages or associations whose authenticity would be apparent to the nation and accepted by it. The fact that in a democracy we do not rely upon our priests to perform this necessary function means not that the function is less obligatory but that it must be performed with scrupulous care by those into whose charge it falls.

I must conclude, therefore, that one of the damning weaknesses of our present system of choosing Presidents is that connivings in either the Electoral College or the House could cast doubts upon the legitimacy of the succession. That is the best single reason for reform. Whatever new system we adopt must add to the visible legitimacy of our government.

Two-party system. Our two-party system is infinitely better than any one-party system so far devised, and considerably better than any three-party system, or twenty-party. Although its roots extend backwards to Greece, its operational perfection is a unique contribution of the Anglo-Saxon political mind, and it functions. It seems to me, after long involvement in rather tough two-party politics, that anything which strengthens this system is good for America and anything which weakens it is bad.

One of the things I have done in politics which seems now to have been more sensible than most came at the end of Hawaii's first general election after the granting of statehood. It was a bitter brawl, a true confrontation between an old, good, powerful, paternal system of government that had run the islands well and autocratically for many generations, and a rambunctious, liberal, somewhat undisciplined, future-looking uprising of groups who no longer wished to be governed in the old patterns. My side lost. But in the days immediately after the heated battle I wrote a series of articles for the local paper, in which I pointed out that the Republican victors would be wise indeed if they found jobs and provided opportunities for the young Democrats who had lost. I advised this on the grounds that sooner or later Hawaii was going to have Democrats in government and it was better to have good ones than bad, to have men who had not been forced to make unwise commitments but who had earned their livelihood in responsible ways that bound them to the community. Today the young Democrats of whom I then spoke help govern Hawaii and sit in Congress to help govern the nation. Today I would tell them the same thing about Republicans; sooner or later Republicans will again be in power in the islands and it will be better for all if they are good Republicans rather than bad.

The more rugged the party battles, the more those who participate in them approve our system of allowing our two parties to assume responsibility for the organizing of our political life. It would be senseless for us to flee the known dangers of the Electoral College only to create the greater dangers of a multi-party system. In order for American government to function, we require strong parties and must introduce no reforms which would weaken them. As a hard-working Democrat I have always felt more at ease with a dedicated Republican than with a wishy-washy Democrat, because the former is essential to my own welfare, whereas the latter may do both me and my nation much damage.

Federalism. Much of our national vitality has derived from the compromises worked out by our Constitutional Convention in 1787 whereby the rights of large and small states were kept in balance. I have lived both in states with few electoral votes, like Hawaii and Colorado, and in large ones, like New York and Ohio, and I know at first hand the inequalities of our system, but I cannot imagine a federal balance more adroitly assembled than ours. The delicate arrangements so painfully worked out should not be upset.

From time to time I have been challenged by my friends regarding this principle of states' rights, and I have myself questioned why a man so liberal in so many areas should in this critical one incline always toward the more conservative view. I believe it stems from my early admiration for Alexander Hamilton and John C. Calhoun, the cerebral senator from South Carolina, who, if he did not coin the phrase, first brought it to my attention: "The minority must be protected from the tyranny of the majority." I know well how this principle led Calhoun into the successive follies of southern partisanship, nullification, and secession, and I know how Calhoun, hewing to the line of this principle, lost in the greatest philosophical debate our Congress has ever engaged in, that led by the federalist Daniel Webster against the states'-rights Calhoun; but I know also that the foundation of Calhoun's thinking was sound and that he enunciated truths which are as vital today as when he spoke them. The main one, I think, was his concern over the tenuous relationships which bind our states and regions together.

I am totally committed to the principle that Hawaii has inherent problems that are different from those of Vermont, and that each has a right to a fair hearing. I believe that the southwest region of our nation has problems which are unlike those of the Boston-to-Richmond belt, and that each must be given due consideration. That our general problems are overriding, no man in his right mind would deny, so that in any Webster-Calhoun debate one must come down firmly on the side of the former; but to ignore Calhoun's fundamental truths about states and regions and minorities is to miss the whole point of American federalism.

What this means in judging any proposed system for electing a President is that I look with suspicion at any proposal which would submerge the fifty individual states into a conglomerate mass, and I tend to prefer systems which take into account the fact that the Mississippi Basin has problems and attitudes rather different from those which operate in California, Oregon, and Washington. To return to an earlier distinction, the fact that I am appalled by the Electoral College and totally determined to do what I can to eliminate it does not mean that I am also opposed to the system of allotting to each of the states the electoral votes to which the latest census entitles them.

When one considers the crises that have grown out of the problem of finding a just system of federalism in nations as disparate as India, Belgium, Nigeria, Indonesia, and even Spain—I am thinking of the Basques and Catalans—one is inclined to advise any nation which has developed a workable system to cling to it and not to modify it capriciously.

With these principles in mind, let us look briefly at four proposals which comprise the major suggestions for reform, but in looking at them let us apply two critical questions which determine whether the plan meets the minimum requirements. Once satisfied on these basic points, we can proceed to consider the refinements. The two questions are:

1. Does this proposed plan abolish the Electoral College?
2. Does this proposed plan end the risk involved when inconclusive elections are thrown into the House of Representatives?

If the proposed plan fails to pass the first test, it can hardly be worth considering; if it fails the second, it still has a chance, depending upon the ingenuity and practicality of the safeguards erected in event of a House election. If any plan fails both tests, it should be discarded at once, for it would merit no one's support.

FOUR SUGGESTED PLANS

The automatic plan. The Electoral College would be abolished. The electoral system would be retained. House elections would be continued, but with marked improvements; under an alternate version they would be avoided by means of run-off elections.

The only honest way to describe this plan is to say that it is our present system, purged of its more glaring weaknesses. Each state and the District of Columbia would continue to have such electoral votes as the census provided, and these would continue to be allocated among the candidates on a winner-take-all basis. There would continue to be a total of 538 electoral votes, with 270 still required for election. The crucial improvement here would be that each state's vote would be transmitted automatically to Congress (via the Administrator of General Services in Washington) without the interposition of the faceless members of the Electoral College. Third-party candidates would thus be forestalled from dictating an election in the College.

Under one version inconclusive elections would still be thrown into the Congress, but with such commendable improvements in voting procedure that the major disadvantages of Congressional election would be diminished if not altogether abolished. If no candidate received the necessary 270 electoral votes, the three top contenders would be presented to a joint session of the House and Senate in which each of the 535 members would have one vote, publicly recorded. The majority necessary for election would be 268 votes, and since three contenders would be involved, a situation might develop in which no man could win this necessary majority. A suggestion has been made that this impasse be avoided by the simple device of permitting a man to win with a bare plurality. In an extreme case the vote for the three contenders could wind up 179–178–178, and I wonder if such a minority choice would enhance the legitimacy of the Presidency or would, indeed, be tolerated by the nation.

A further weakness of the Congressional election as the plan was originally proposed was that if the vote went to the joint session of Senate and House, the District of Columbia would be disfranchised, and since it has a greater population than eleven of the states (Alaska, Delaware, Hawaii, Idaho, Montana, Nevada, New Hampshire, North Dakota, South Dakota, Vermont, Wyoming), this could hardly be defended. A later version of the plan, however, corrected this by proposing that when the House and Senate convened, the electoral votes allotted to the District of Columbia (at present three) be awarded automatically to that candidate who had carried the District. The weakness of this is twofold: The District would have no living persons representing it in the give-and-take of the joint session, where human factors can be so crucial; and there could well be a situation in which the District had been carried by a candidate who did not place among the top three, in which case it would again be disfranchised. I am sure that adjustments could be made to solve this intricate technical problem and I do not judge it to be a disqualifying drawback. Certainly, voters in the District of Columbia have a right to share in electing the President.

Under the latest refinement of this plan, House elections would be avoided by a twofold reform. A candidate could win if he led the field with 40 per cent of the electoral vote; and if no one gained that percentage, a run-off election would be held between the two top contenders. The first half of this innovation is most radical, in that 40 per cent of the electoral vote could be produced by a pronounced minority of the popular vote. Once again we would face the situation in which the candidate who had won the popular vote was denied the Presidency, and the principle of legitimacy would have been abused.

If one now looks at the automatic plan with its various corrections, he sees that the virtues of this limited reform are many. It preserves the good parts of our traditional system while correcting the bad. It respects the federal compromise between small states and large. By emphasizing the vote in large states like California and Pennsylvania, it permits cities like Los Angeles and Philadelphia to exercise a legitimate leverage, which offsets the advantages that have customarily accrued to rural areas. Also, the winner-take-all feature discourages the growth of splinter parties. Some critics have depreciated my next point, but it is nevertheless one which makes much sense to me: the fact that a small difference in the popular vote is usually magnified into a more conspicuous difference in the electoral vote produces an illusion that the victor won by a more definitive margin than he actually won by, and this makes it easier for the loser to accept. Kennedy's minuscule margin in 1960 was thus magnified, as was Nixon's slightly larger margin in 1968, and in each instance I, for one, was gratified that the final results looked as clear-cut as they did. To such reasoning, Senator Margaret Chase Smith responds, "Of all the arguments made by the defenders of the Electoral College, I find this to be the most fatuous and guilty of sheer sophistry." I of course would reply that I make it not in defense of the Electoral College, for which I could never say a good word, but of the electoral system, for which I could say many.

Finally, in spite of the blatant miscarriages to which I have already alluded—Adams-Jackson in 1824 and Hayes-Tilden in 1876—and in spite of the fact that fifteen of our Presidents have been elected with less than a majority of the popular votes, the fact remains that the system has worked. Pragmatically speaking, it has been a great success, having outlasted several hundred other governmental systems that have been tried in other nations in the period since 1789.

A surprising number of serious students of American history advise holding onto our present plan because in spite of its weaknesses it accomplishes much. Historian Carl Becker pointed out that the electoral system is a major factor in forcing both political parties to keep close to the middle of the road so as to pick up votes from all varied parts of the nation. It also prevents parties from taking exaggerated stands which might inflame certain levels of the population across the nation, producing a kind of political hysteria.

Clinton Rossiter, historian and educator, is another who is dubious about change. He warns that "we should hesitate a long time before replacing a humpty-dumpty system that works with a neat one that will blow up in our faces."

The most powerful voice in favor of keeping the electoral system was President John F. Kennedy, who while still a senator pointed out that it prevents any one region of the nation from attaining too much power and also retains a workable plan of checks and balances. On the whole, said Kennedy, it has given us "able Presidents capable of meeting the increased demands upon our Executive. No urgent necessity for immediate change has been proven." In debate on March 5, 1956, he argued, "The point I want to make is that when all these factors are considered, it is not only the unit vote for the Presidency we are talking about, but a whole solar system of governmental power. If it is proposed to change the balance of power of one of the elements of the solar system, it is necessary to consider all the others. . . . I am very strongly opposed to any change in the Constitution at this time. The present system has served us well. Its advantages are well known. But the consequences of the proposed amendment, however desirable they may appear to be, cannot be foretold."

Arguments against continuing the present system, even with the improvements suggested, are formidable and have been discussed at length in the preceding chapter. Critics stress the accidental derivation of the system, its winner-take-all tradition, the pusillanimity of the electors, the domination by the two parties, and the power accorded to minorities. They argue persuasively that a plan with so many defects ought to be scrapped altogether in favor of a carefully worked out plan which reforms the entire system.

Opponents also advance certain technical objections to the present system. Conclusive legal results of a November election ought to be known more quickly than they can be now. It is ridiculous to postpone the electoral voting till mid-December, and the Congressional solution of deadlocked elections until January of the following year. A very telling attack is one whose merit will become clear when we study Appendix C and the explanations which accompany it; briefly, the present system, contrary to popular belief, produces a considerable advantage for large states and thus poses a threat to the federal system rather than being a prop for it.

One technical objection to the automatic plan merits careful consideration. If the kind of constitutional amendment which the advocates of this plan propose is adopted, a fundamental change will have been made inadvertently in our system without our having been aware of the consequences. The amendment would freeze into permanent form the winner-take-all tradition which is now merely the creature of the fifty state legislatures. To change the amendment would require approval of both the Senate and House by two-thirds majorities plus a ratification by three fourths of the states; to change the tradition as it now exists would require only action by the various legislatures, or the courts. This point will become of added significance when the data of Appendix C are explored, for then the inadvisability of freezing into permanent form the source of grave inequity will be demonstrated.

The district plan. The Electoral College would be retained. Inconclusive elections would continue to be thrown into Congress. But in each process innovative safeguards would be added to forestall fraud.

Each state and the District of Columbia would continue to have its allotted number of electoral votes, but they would be applied in a striking new way. In California, for example, the 38 votes corresponding to that state's 38 House members would be decided not in a mass on a winner-take-all basis as at present, but separately in each of 38 districts, not necessarily identical with the Congressional districts. The two other votes, representing California's two senators, would be decided at large from the entire state.

Note what a significant change this would introduce. In 1968 the popular vote was quite close in California—3,467,644 to 3,244,318—but because the Republicans finished 223,326 votes ahead, Nixon garnered all 40 electoral votes and Humphrey none. Had the state voted by districts, plus two votes at large, the count would probably have been 23 to 17 in favor of Nixon, even though California's House delegation, elected from those same districts, divided 21 to 17 Democratic.

The problem of an irresponsible Electoral College would be avoided in an interesting way. Each would-be elector would take a pledge to vote the way his state voted, and since this provision would then become part of the Constitution, it could be enforced by law, whereas now it cannot be. If he voted contrary to his pledge, such vote would be ignored and "counted as a vote cast in accordance with his declaration."

To become President, a candidate would still have to win an absolute majority of the Electoral College—at present, 270 votes—but in the event that all the votes are evenly divided between two candidates—at present this would be 269 each—that candidate who had won the largest number of individual districts would be the winner. If more than two candidates split the electoral vote in such a way that no one had a majority, the inconclusive election would be thrown into the Congress, but with two distinct improvements. The Senate would meet with the House in joint session, as explained in the previous proposal, and all members would vote as individuals, an absolute majority being required—at present, 268 votes. (As the proposal now stands, no provision is made for the District of Columbia, hence the figure of 268, but, as discussed before, this could easily be rectified.) The second improvement is unique to this proposal. Since three candidates would be contending in the joint House-Senate session, a situation would be possible in which no one of them could win a majority; if on the first ballot such a deadlock developed, on the second ballot only the two candidates who had stood first and second on the first ballot would be voted upon, and this would produce a winner unless absentees or abstentions made a decision impossible, but rules for voting could be passed which would prevent such a tactic.

A major argument in favor of this plan is its long association with American history. In the early years of our nation a number of states selected their electors on the district plan; Jefferson, Hamilton, Madison, J. Q. Adams, Jackson, Van Buren, and Webster all championed this idea. It was proposed often as a nationwide obligation and was passed by the Senate four different times between 1813 and 1824. In 1820 it failed to win House approval by only five votes. Left to their own free choice of methods for selecting electors, individual states continued to follow the district plan, Michigan returning to it as late as 1892. Of the three new proposals—district, proportional, direct—only the first has ever been a tested part of the American procedure for electing Presidents.

Proponents of the plan cite a long list of advantages that would flow from it. A President so chosen would more nearly reflect the total composition of the nation, in that each resident of each district would have the same vote as the resident of every other district in the nation, namely, three votes, two for the electors representing the two senators and one for the elector representing the representatives. In effect, the nation would be composed of 436 small states of comparable population and more or less comparable influence. (The total number of votes, of course, would be 538 because of the addition of 102 at-large votes—2 from each state and from the District of Columbia.)

It would diminish the importance of a few large states and would mean that a Presidential candidate might logically be chosen from almost any part of the nation. The two-party system would be encouraged in that no matter what the preponderance of registration in a given state, there would always be a chance for the minority party to pick off an elector here and there, a possibility not available in the winner-take-all system.

The sponsors realize that the district plan would be an invitation for the various state legislatures to gerrymander—especially since districts need not conform to Congressional districts but can be drawn to taste—but a limited safeguard has been introduced forbidding the legislature from redistricting until a new census has been taken. The fact that district lines would be altered after most censuses, whether Congressional lines were followed or not, would make the selection of electors more responsive to population shifts, and this would be desirable.

Specifically, the district plan would diminish the influence of minorities centered in cities, since their swing votes would influence only the electoral vote of their district and not the total vote of their state. For this reason the plan has usually been considered advantageous to rural areas as opposed to urban, to small states as opposed to large, to the more conservative elements of our society as opposed to the radical.

There seems to be little doubt that in the 1950s when this plan was seriously revived, it would have been a most powerful weapon for controlling cities and augmenting rural strength, for in those days prior to the Supreme Court's decision in *Baker v. Carr* and the enunciation of the one-man–one-vote doctrine, the Congressional districts of this nation grossly favored the rural areas and even more grossly penalized the cities. If the districts of 1956 were still in operation, this plan would be an intolerable steal and no sensible large state or urban area would tolerate it; but with the new districts drawn in conformity to Supreme Court decisions, the old discrepancies have been largely eliminated and the district plan is to be taken seriously.

Opponents of the plan have been outspoken. They argue that in spite of pious avowals to the contrary, the gerrymandering of districts would become such a fine art that no court could keep up with the innovations. Only one who has lived in a notoriously gerrymandered district, as I have, can appreciate the cynical effectiveness of this device in controlling elections. I would judge that if you gave me and my Democratic cronies a free hand, we could gerrymander a swing state like Pennsylvania so that its 27 House seats in Congress, now divided 14–13 Democratic, would be divided under our plan into something like 16 Democrats to 11 Republicans, whereas a bunch of Republican experts could take the same census figures and come up with something like 15 Republicans to 12 Democrats. I shudder to think of what the Massachusetts or Texas legislatures could do to their states, and this plan seems an invitation to such skulduggery. The creative contribution of minority groups—forcing candidates to take them seriously, probably to the benefit of the nation—would be lost. Urban problems could more easily be shunted aside, since the cities would have lost much of their power, and splinter parties would proliferate, each hoping to win enough votes to strike a balance of power which could be exerted—if not in the Electoral College, in the joint session of Congress.

One aspect of the plan is problematic. When pointing out that as defined at present the plan would disfranchise the District of Columbia whenever the election went to the Congress, I said with a certain optimism that this defect could be easily rectified. Now I am not so sure. When one considers the conservative nature of the sponsors of this plan, one gains the suspicion that they might not want to give the District, which contains a preponderant Negro population, any concessions and that the plan could well be used to deny the District rights to which it is entitled.

Finally, if it were imprudent to freeze into the Constitution the relatively mild provisions of the automatic plan, how much more so would be the continuance of constitutional authorization for the electors, which this plan would ensure?

The long-time champion of this reform has been Senator Karl Mundt, of South Dakota, who has said, "The Electoral College, operating under the rule of 'winner-take-all,' is, in my estimation, the most unfair, inaccurate, uncertain, and undemocratic institution of all." He has argued persuasively through many years that his district plan will bring democracy back to the College.

The National Association of Manufacturers has supported this plan, as have the Daughters of the American Revolution, H. L. Hunt of Texas, and Senators Goldwater of Arizona, Thurmond of South Carolina, Tower of Texas, Hruska of Nebraska, Stennis and Eastland of Mississippi, Miller of Iowa, Williams of Delaware, Jordan of Idaho, and Hansen of Wyoming, among others.

The proportional plan. The Electoral College would be abolished. The electoral system would be retained. Inconclusive elections would continue to be thrown into Congress, but with notable safeguards.

Each state and the District of Columbia would continue to have its apportioned electoral votes. They would be allocated, however, not on the winner-take-all system as at present but according to the proportional vote gained by each candidate, carried to three decimal places and disregarding the fourth. If this plan had been in operation in 1968, the California vote would not have been Nixon 40, Humphrey 0, Wallace 0, others 0; but Nixon 19.127, Humphrey 17.895, Wallace 2.687, others 0.288. These results would have been transmitted automatically to the Congress. The virtue of this plan is that it permits minority votes to exercise leverage rather than to be submerged in a one-party victory. Even if a minority party knows it cannot win the entire state, it can work hard for its fair share of the electoral votes. The drawback to the plan, of course, is that the opportunity this provides encourages third parties and even nineteenth and twentieth parties, each trusting that it will be able to pick up a few electoral votes here and there. Obviously, if enough minority parties in the fifty states picked up enough stray votes, most Presidential elections would be thrown into the House. Our elections would prove inconclusive and America would face the problem of fragmentation which has stricken so many other democracies.

To avoid this, proponents suggest that if the leading candidate wins as many as 40 per cent of the electoral votes, he will be declared the winner. If no candidate wins 40 per cent, the top two candidates—not three, as in the preceding plans—would be presented to a joint session of the House and Senate, voting as individual members, and they would elect the next President. Since the combined membership is 535, a vote of 268 would be required to elect. As in the case of the earlier plans, this one disfranchises the District of Columbia whenever the decision goes to Congress, an omission which could be rectified; and as before, elections in Congress would be open to sabotage by absenteeism or abstention.

Proportionalism was formally proposed to Congress as early as 1848, and through the years, picked up the support of senators like Henry Cabot Lodge of Massachusetts, who has long been the chief proponent of the plan, Sparkman of Alabama, Pell of Rhode Island, Smathers of Florida, Kuchel of California, Saltonstall of Massachusetts, and Dodd of Connecticut. In 1950 enough Senate support had been generated to pass the proposal, but in the House it was rejected, 134–210. Had it been approved by the latter body and then submitted to the states as an amendment, no one can now judge whether it would have been ratified or not, but it is the only one of the four plans that has had any serious chance of acceptance in recent decades.

Arguments in favor of proportionalism range all the way from those enthusiastic ideas that used to populate high school debates to some of the gravest considerations voiced by political philosophers in recent years. The proportional plan provides the nearest practical approach to direct popular voting while at the same time retaining the historic principle of according each state its allotted electoral votes. It thus conserves the best traditions of the nation.

Under this plan the electoral vote would conform somewhat more closely to the actual popular vote than it does at present, and after the election the voters would have before them a better approximation of the relative strengths of all the parties, since now the majority party receives a swollen bank statement and the smaller minority parties none at all. Also, this plan would diminish the effectiveness of swing minority groups in the largest states in that by swinging they would control not the entire vote of their states but only a just proportion of that vote.

One claim has been made which I am not competent to appraise. It is said that this plan would diminish the effectiveness, and therefore the likelihood, of fraud, in that the contaminated votes would affect not the whole electoral vote of a state but only the relative proportion. If this proved to be true, it would be a valuable asset in our political life, for in recent elections the conduct in various states has been questionable, and anything that can be done to quarantine the impact of such fraud and keep it from infecting the whole system is to be commended. I consider this a much more serious problem than I used to and point out that the district plan would also provide a commendable quarantine safeguard.

Since the principal objection to the proportional plan is its encouragement to minority parties, whose proliferation would corrupt our political system, the proponents have been at great pains to assuage fears in this respect. They claim that the safeguard against such proliferation is the provision that a candidate can win with only 40 per cent of the electoral vote, which would mean that the minority parties could not hope to throw very many inconclusive elections into the Congress.

Senator Sparkman has summed up other assets of the plan which he has long championed: "Proportionate division of the electoral vote according to the popular vote in each state would require candidates to give attention to the issues of interest to citizens in all areas of the country. Likewise, it would broaden the eligibility of candidates who are not from the majority party of a large state, and would eliminate the neglect of smaller states that are inclined to favor one party consistently." (At the 1969 session of Congress, Senator Sparkman appeared as a sponsor for Senator Mundt's district plan.)

Opponents of the plan have naturally focused on its invitation to splinter parties, and the reader will have to make up his own mind on this question, there being ample testimony on both sides. A charge which in the long run might prove more serious is that the introduction of proportionalism in Presidential elections would establish a precedent for its introduction throughout the rest of our political life, producing chaos in certain state, county, and municipal operations.

Critics point to a serious technical impediment which would arise whenever there was a close election, and many recent ones have fallen into that category, with a likelihood that those ahead may do so too. Under our present system the total vote of a state need be only approximate in order to indicate which way that state's electoral votes will go, and a conclusive result of the national vote can be known even though the specific vote of numerous states is still undetermined. Under the proportional plan the state count would have to be reasonably complete and accurate before the proper proportions could be calculated and distributed. Approximations could not be used, since the proportions must be carried to the third decimal place. (As we shall see shortly, if this plan had been in operation in 1960, victory would have depended upon 0.452, or less than half, of a vote, and this result could not have been known accurately for weeks after the election in view of absentee ballots, delayed counts, and contested results.)

Other critics argue that although proportionalism is a step toward direct popular voting, it fails because it continues to award the smallest states with their two automatic electoral votes corresponding to their two senators. At present those two votes are more than often offset by the winner-take-all tradition, as we shall see (page 96); but if the winner-take-all formula is destroyed by proportionalism, the value of the two automatic votes accruing to small states becomes enormous. These critics insist that if one is willing to take a token step toward a direct popular vote, he ought to be willing to go the whole way. The merits of whatever plan one proposes must be weighed against the merits of a completely popular, direct vote. When this is done, argue the proponents of direct voting, the advantages lie all in favor of the direct vote, and proportionalism is seen as a pallid substitute.

Defenders of proportionalism dismiss this reasoning by pointing out that in politics no argument *reductio ad absurdum* is impressive. The fact that a little concession to direct popular voting is good does not necessarily mean that a total move in that direction would be better. Perhaps the degree of popular voting provided by the proportional plan is the precise amount required.

Direct popular vote. The Electoral College, the accidental electoral system, and the throwing of inconclusive elections into the House would all be abolished.

The only factor that would be involved in electing a President would be the actual number of votes cast throughout the nation. Theoretically, a man's vote in a remote Arizona village would count precisely as much as one cast on Park Avenue in New York, and no state would have an accidental advantage over any other.

In an effort to reduce the likelihood of inconclusive elections, a candidate would be permitted to win with only 40 per cent of the total popular vote, and if no one gained that percentage, an immediate run-off election between the two leading candidates would be held, which would mean that no future elections could ever be thrown into the House, nor into a joint session of House and Senate.

The merits of this plan have become increasingly attractive as a result of recent experiences. A principal advantage is that with one sweep of the broom the conglomeration of past accidents and errors would be swept away; electors, weighted voting, the power of minority blocs, the disparity between states, inconclusive elections, and the dread confusion of House elections would be abolished, once and for all. There would be a clean break with such impedimenta of the past as electors and House elections, but the essential values of historical procedures, such as a free vote and an independent President, would be respected and preserved. Above all, our citizens would then vote according to a system all of whose parts they understood, which yielded clear-cut results, and which enhanced the visible legitimacy of the succession to the Presidency.

Especially persuasive is the argument that since the President is the leader of all the people of the nation, he should be elected by them without the interposition of either electors or devices which might frustrate the expressed will of the people. Since the electoral system has been in operation forty-six Presidential elections have been held, and in fifteen the man declared winner has received less than half the votes cast. In this century five such elections, four Democratic and one Republican, have occurred: Wilson 41.85; Wilson 49.26; Truman 49.51; Kennedy 49.71; Nixon 43.40.

And three times the ultimate winner has not only won the Presidency with less than a majority; he has even got fewer votes than his opponent. In other words, the man with the highest vote was declared the loser. In 1824 Andrew Jackson won but John Quincy Adams was named President. In 1876 Samuel J. Tilden won by more than a quarter of a million votes, a substantial margin in those days, but lost the Presidency to Rutherford B. Hayes. And in 1888 Grover Cleveland won by 95,096 votes but lost to Benjamin Harrison.

In each instance the stability of the nation was preserved because of the good sportsmanship of the loser, even though some might have sympathized if he had shouted "Foul!" and tried to rally his supporters to contest the results. In the Hayes-Tilden fracas, as we have seen, the winner was not designated until two days before the inauguration, and there were many who feared that the same kind of impasse might be repeated in 1969. The advocates of a direct vote argue, "In the past we have been lucky. We should not depend upon such luck indefinitely."

It is obvious that under each of the preceding three plans it would be possible, whenever an election was thrown into the Congress, for a candidate to lose even though he had clearly won the popular vote. Would it not be simpler, ask the advocates of this plan, to have a straightforward election in which the voters knew exactly what they were doing and in which the results stood forth clearly? This would avoid the national disgust that might arise if a popular winner were deprived by Congress of his victory.

A final group of reasons for supporting direct popular voting is that it would permit the small states to play a more active role in electing a President. The small states have begun to suspect that the two electoral votes given them for their two senators, regardless of the size of the state, are an illusory advantage which actually works to their disadvantage, and as we shall see when we consider the data summarized in Appendix C, they are right. As a matter of fact, perhaps the strongest single argument in favor of direct popular voting is that it would redress the balance of power among the various states.

Even so, opponents of direct popular voting still argue that it would rupture the historic compact made between the small and large states and would thus destroy the federal principle. A practical corollary is that since the small states would apparently be penalized, it is futile even to discuss the plan because an amendment requires the approval of three fourths of the states, and this would never be forthcoming. This argument, of course, is made in ignorance of the true relationship between the small and large states, a situation which I shall discuss in detail later.

A curious technical objection is that direct popular voting would severely penalize those states in which it is not the custom for large numbers of eligible citizens to register, or to vote if they are registered. For example, if two states A and B each have a population of 10,000,000 and consequently the same 26 electoral votes, under our present system it does not really matter if 4,500,000 vote in state A and only 200,000 in state B, for regardless of how large the popular vote is, or how it differs between A and B, in the end both states will cast the same number of electoral votes. Under the direct plan, however, a state would contribute only those votes which were actually cast, and if the voters of State B failed to exercise their franchise, or were prevented from doing so, that state would penalize itself. Without being invidious, let me offer a few comparisons from the close election of 1960 and the reader can form his own conclusions as to the merits of this objection:

Voting percentages
in eight representative states
1960 Presidential Election
(figures rounded)

State	Population of Voting Age	Votes Cast	Percentage	Electoral Vote
Alabama	1,834,000	570,000	31.1	11
Connecticut	1,591,000	1,223,000	76.8	8
Georgia	2,410,000	733,000	30.4	12
Indiana	2,778,000	2,135,000	76.9	13
Minnesota	2,001,000	1,542,000	77.0	11
Mississippi	1,171,000	298,000	25.5	8
Virginia	2,313,000	771,000	33.4	12
Wisconsin	2,354,000	1,729.000	73.4	12

It will be observed that in 1960 it took only 570,000 voters in Alabama to cast 11 electoral votes, whereas in Minnesota it required more than two and a half times that number to achieve the same result. The discrepancy between Mississippi and Connecticut, each with eight electoral votes, was even greater. Direct voting would end this injustice. If a state voted its people, it would exercise leverage; if it made voting difficult or impossible, it would lose thereby.

The next objection can be extrapolated from the table just offered. If all that counted in an election were the direct popular vote, all states would be forced to adopt voting qualifications equal to the most liberal permitted in any one state. For example, if State A allowed its citizens to vote at age eighteen, and thus qualified a large number so as to influence the choice of President, the other fifty jurisdictions in self-defense would have to do likewise. At this point State B might come up with a clever innovation which the others would have to match. To stop this kind of basement bargaining, federal laws would pretty surely be required, and they would dictate such things as voting age, registration procedures, and polling practices. Opponents of federal control hold that this is too high a price to pay for the admitted advantages that otherwise flow from direct popular voting.

Another objection is that this plan would favor the large cities and would force candidates to spend most of their time fighting for the cities as now they fight for the large states. Enhancing the importance of the cities would also increase the importance of minority groups, who would thus surrender their old leverage in the state for a new one in the city.

As to the claim of the proponents that this plan would diminish the frequency of close or ambiguous elections, opponents cite the comment of President Truman, who pointed out, "There is something to be said for the narrow margin of victory in a Presidential election. It makes the new President realize . . . that there is more than one side to a question." The voices and ideas of the millions who voted for the loser should be "just as important [to the President-elect] as those of the victorious millions."

Senator Spessard Holland of Florida, in a comment given in 1967, spelled out his good reasons for opposing direct popular voting. He pointed out that since the District of Columbia would under this plan gain more voting power than the eleven states cited before, the plan would be unfair in that the District "does not have any of the duties or responsibilities of sovereign statehood." One staunch defender of the District, and a proponent of direct voting, replied, "This would make the accident of residence or employment with the federal government a justification for depriving citizens of their right to vote according to the ancient principle that it is geographical areas that have the right to representation and not human beings. Since this doctrine was used for nearly two centuries to inhibit the rights of urban areas, and since its effect was deleterious to our states, it should hardly be used as a guiding principle for our federal union."

The general public is strongly in favor of direct popular voting. Polls taken over the last few years have produced these striking results: 1966—63 per cent in favor; 1967—65 per cent; 1968, before the election—79 per cent; 1968, after the election—81 per cent.

Experts also favor this plan. In 1966 Senator Quentin N. Burdick of North Dakota polled more than 8,000 members of our fifty state legislatures, and those who responded voted as follows: keep the existing system, 9.7 per cent; adopt the district system, 10.2 per cent; adopt the proportional system, 21.2 per cent; abolish all parts of the electoral system and adopt instead a direct popular vote, 58.8 per cent.

Many American leaders have recommended the direct vote: the American Bar Association, the Federal Bar Association, former Governors Branigin of Indiana and Brown of California, and Senators Morse, Mansfield, Aiken, Keating, and Margaret Chase Smith, who has been a constant proponent: "From the long term aspect, the Electoral College is doomed to be replaced by the direct popular election system. It is only a matter of time. For the American people will ultimately assert themselves and demand that the will of the majority prevail."

Today the major champion is Senator Birch Bayh of Indiana, who has been conducting a vigorous campaign in favor of this plan. He summarizes his argument as follows: "For all practical purposes, the outcome of Presidential elections today is determined by a small group of marginal voters in eleven or twelve large, politically doubtful states. By inflating the value of these individual popular votes, our Presidential machinery effectively denies to millions of Americans an equal opportunity to affect the outcome of Presidential elections. Under any system of winner-take-all formula, we face the prospect of elevating to the Presidency a man who is not the popular choice of the American people."

Shortly after the 1968 election I had an opportunity to discuss Presidential elections with Hubert H. Humphrey, and in the aftermath of defeat he made these observations: "I would have been perfectly willing to place my political destiny directly in the hands of the voters of this nation. Our President and our Vice-President are our only two truly national figures elected by all the people of the nation, and the process should be turned over to all the people.

"What is the Electoral College if you analyze it? An American House of Lords with even less function, except to do great damage. Why should we run the risk of having these irresponsible men and women engage in brokerage over our choice of President?

"Why not come clean? Why not do the right thing? Let us stop this playing for a few large states and throw the election of our principal officials open to the honest vote of the entire population."

These conclusions surprised me somewhat, for Humphrey at one time favored a form of the proportional plan and defended it ably when he was in the Senate. Of this he said, "Sure I was for the plan then. It's a good plan with admirable features, but the more I study the structure of our nation, and the complexities of our elections, the more strongly I incline toward a straight popular vote."

In concluding, Humphrey said with great emphasis, "I wish to make one point especially clear. The federal system which we all prize has nothing to do with the electoral system. Its integrity does not depend upon our continuing to award each state two electoral votes for its two senators. That is a complete misconception. The heart of our federal system lies in the fact that the United States Senate is supposed to protect the interests of all the states, so that smaller ones cannot be ignored, while in the House of Representatives the large states have a voting power which protects their interests. That's the federal system and not a bunch of electoral votes. As a matter of fact, the present electoral system damages the federal system because it permits the large states to exercise an undue leverage on our Presidential elections. If you want to preserve the basic functions of our federal system, go to a direct popular vote."

Advocates of such a plan conclude with a line of reasoning which is impressive from the historical point of view: Consider the nation both as a whole and as a sum of parts. The whole consists of all of us across the entire nation. We should operate as a whole and in a direct popular vote elect a President who stands for all of us. The part labeled state will be represented by the two senators elected from the entire state. And the part labeled district, with its cities and towns and villages, will be represented by the House of Representatives elected from those districts. The union of these three elements—nation, state, district, each represented in its own way—would form the most viable and balanced system of government that could be devised. Perhaps this is the new federalism, with accretions that had gathered about the old scraped away.

TWO GENERAL IMPROVEMENTS

Before trying to determine which of the four proposed reforms is best, we should look briefly at two other suggested improvements which would fit equally well with any of the proposals.

National primary. Under this system qualified voters in all states would go to the polls on a given day in late spring or early summer, the Republicans taking one ballot, the Democrats another, and they would indicate the men they preferred to run for President and Vice-President on their respective tickets. The value of this plan would be that the people themselves would be nominating the men they wanted, rather than leaving that task to conventions of the two parties, where popular preferences are often submerged by political leaders who dominate the conventions. The weakness is that this plan would diminish the importance of the two political parties, which in the long run are responsible for our political life and which generally have done a good job. Under the convention system, the toughest political minds of this nation scrutinize potential contenders for four years and isolate the strengths and weaknesses of these men. A nationwide primary would tend to degenerate into a popularity contest in which one flashy television speech, one quick reaction to an emergency might sway the nation, producing a result no one had intended or even anticipated. This, of course, is a danger in any direct popular vote, and it was to avoid this danger that the electoral system was introduced. Those favoring a national primary argue that our society is now sufficiently advanced and sophisticated to be immune to such temporary fervors.

There is one enormous virtue to the proposed national primary. Today one man alone, the President-nominate, decides by his own authority who the next Vice-President shall be, and frequently the man thus arbitrarily designated becomes President. He has reached the highest office in the land on the vote of one man, and this ought to be stopped.

Shorter election campaigns. The Presidential campaign now runs a full twelve months, from November of one year to November of the next, and this is cruelly wasteful, particularly since the scattered primaries in which the candidates engage are inconclusive. Senator Eugene McCarthy won various primaries but this did not ensure him even serious attention at the Chicago convention.

In a recent poll, voters across the nation indicated that they favored cutting the campaign time in half—60 per cent in favor, 13 per cent undecided—and said they thought we would not lose any conspicuous advantages if this were done.

Also there must be a general overhaul of the party conventions. The Democrats, at least, could not afford another debacle like the one they engineered at Chicago, for this transformed them overnight from leaders in the campaign to underdogs.

V

WHAT MUST
BE DONE
NOW

WITH THE NATION AGITATED BY ITS NARROW ESCAPE FROM chaos in the election of 1968, with polls showing 81 per cent of the population favoring remedial action, and with leaders throughout the nation warning that we must take steps now to avert disaster later on, one would naturally assume that reform would be easily attained. One would expect that Congress, having agreed that the Electoral College and House election must be abolished, would proceed to debate the merits of the four alternate plans, and each house would pass the agreed-upon improvement by the two-thirds vote that is required. The proposed amendment would then go to the states, and since popular support for reform has been shown to be really overwhelming, we could look forward to a prompt roll call of states, and by 1971 or early 1972 the thirty-eighth state would have ratified the amendment, which would thereupon become law.

If that sequence were followed, in 1972 we could be choosing our next President by a more rational procedure than we have used in the past, but I am afraid this hope is a delusion.

Ted Lewis, the well-informed political columnist whose job it is to keep a jaundiced eye on Congress, concludes, from studies he has made in Washington, that there is little chance "that the antiquated

Electoral College system will be done away with before the 1972 national campaign." He reasons that "no Congress, whether controlled by Democrats or Republicans, is going to act on the revision issue" until some "horrendous foul-up has actually taken place." The fact that we skinned by safely this time, reasons Lewis, will be adequate excuse for postponing action.

If we allow things to drift, if we take the pressure off Congress, and above all, if we as individuals slip back into apathy, the old sloppy ways will be continued. Left to its own schedule, Congress would hardly get around to a simple action like abolishing the Electoral College, while a radical improvement like terminating House elections, which would in a sense be diminishing its own powers, would not happen. As for choosing among the four alternatives, in the normal course Congress would defer the decision for another fifteen or twenty years, or until, as Mr. Lewis suggests, some horrendous foul-up has occurred.

If we as citizens do nothing, the process of electing a President in 1972 will exactly duplicate the one we used in 1968, and in monotonous sequence the others will follow—1976, 1980, and 1984—each with its built-in propensity for disaster. The apathy of the public, after its latest scare subsides, will support Congress in its avoidance of the issue.

But we can do something. We can insist that at least the most grievous errors of our present system be corrected, and at once. We can keep unrelenting pressure upon Congress until these vital and relatively simple reforms are accomplished. If at the same time we can solve the whole problem, so much the better, but aspiring to a total solution must not detract us from the main business at hand. This is what we can do.

> Step I. We must insist that Congress put into motion immediately the machinery necessary for a constitutional amendment which would abolish the Electoral College and make it possible for states to report the disposition of their electoral votes directly to the Administrator of General Services in Washington.

Since I know of no serious student who proposes that we retain the Electoral College in its present form, and since its retention is not required in any of the alternative systems so far proposed (it is not essential to the operation of the district plan, even though that plan currently proposes its retention as a historical form), I should think that there is a good chance that this vital reform can be achieved.

If it be argued that passing such an amendment would appease the pressures for real reform and thus delay substantial study and decision, I can only reply that the dangers inherent in retaining the present College are so fundamental that they must be terminated, even at the cost of losing a more complete reform. I know how tempting it is to quote from Viscount John Morley's essay "On Compromise": "The small reform may become the enemy of the great one," but ridding ourselves of those lesser errors which would be eliminated by a major reform is not vital; getting rid of the Electoral College is. Of course I would like to see a total overhauling of our archaic system. Of course I would prefer to see my preferred plan adopted, for I would like to see an honest balance struck between the various contending interests of our society. But I would not be willing to gain any of these goals at the cost of keeping our present Electoral College one day longer. Therefore I conclude that speed and decision are necessary.

If it be argued that passing such an amendment would freeze into the Constitution for the time being various accidental aspects of the electoral system, I would be willing to do this in the faith that at some future time further change, much of it corrective, would be made. And if it were not, I deem the price we would have paid for elimination of the Electoral College to have been within reason. We have lived with the present electoral system for nearly two hundred years and I would not object to seeing aspects of it frozen into the Constitution, since they could be unfrozen later on, as was done with Prohibition.

When I spoke with Vice-President Humphrey, he raised the interesting point that perhaps the Electoral College as it exists now could be safeguarded by statute law in a compact between the states rather than by constitutional amendment, requiring electors to vote according to the way their states voted. If this could be done, and could be made binding, which current laws of this nature are not, I would accept this as a stop-gap but I would not be easy with it. As long as the 538 electors exist, as long as they have legal sanction, so long will they be a potential menace. I can think of more than a few figures in our national history who would not have hesitated to browbeat, corrupt, imprison, or otherwise manipulate the electors in order to attain the Presidency. Imagine what Adolf Hitler would have been able to do in 1933 with such a tenuous body! Suppose our nation is badly fragmented politically in 1972 or 1976, then picture the temptation to manipulate this College, especially since to do so would be perfectly legal under our present rules.

I can see no justification for temporizing with this ridiculous instrument a day longer. It must be abolished. It must be abolished now. And it must be abolished by constitutional amendment. We should get on with the task. If we work hard we can achieve it in time for the 1972 election.

When this has been accomplished—or when the path to its accomplishment is clearly seen—we must attend to the second critical problem.

> **Step II. We must insist that Congress put into motion immediately the machinery necessary for a constitutional amendment which would terminate the process whereby inconclusive elections are thrown to the House of Representatives.**

Not even among the small states who would profit from this bizarre plan do I find any serious defense of it as it operates at present, and since its retention is not required in any of the alternative plans (although election by both House and Senate meeting in joint session is), I should think that there is a good chance that this totally unfair and unmanageable type of election can be abolished.

Even though I exercise all the impartiality at my command, I cannot find a single justification for continuing this dangerous system in which each state has one vote and in which a tie vote within a state delegation disfranchises that entire state. This is an eighteenth-century folly which may then have been excusable as a compromise but which now has no justification. We must abolish it.

Fortunately, we have two excellent escapes. The first has considerable merit in that it would preserve all of the present system that is good and eliminate all that is bad. I mean the system whereby inconclusive elections would be thrown not into the House voting by states but into the House and Senate meeting jointly and voting as 535 individuals. I can see nothing wrong with this, and I have examined all possibilities with a microscope. The rights of the minority party are preserved. The rights of small states are guaranteed, because they will still have two senators voting. There is no advantage that I can see to either Republican or Democrat, except insofar as the election has sent more of one to Congress than the other, which is a just discrepancy. It is efficient, is easy to administer, and it would produce a President on the first ballot if a plurality were permitted.

I would like to point out one considerable advantage. Although the system would produce tremendous pressures on the members of Congress, this pressure would be directed at duly elected public officials who must in the future go back to their constituencies for further support; today that same pressure could be applied in a close election to members of the Electoral College, who are not known to the public or responsible to it in any way. I do not believe that congressmen are better men than electors; they are precisely the same kind of men and therefore just as susceptible to pressure and venality. But they are in the public eye and are vulnerable to public discipline; therefore they are better men to gamble on in a crucial situation which can turn fluid at any moment. I do not prefer congressmen to electors because the former are more honest; I prefer them because they can be more easily punished if they turn dishonest.

The other alternative is a run-off election between the two top contenders. This has much to commend it and is, I would judge, the best of all the plans. True, it delays decision, but it produces a clear-cut one. True, it extends an already long campaign by another two to four weeks, but it brings that campaign to a clean, crisp ending. The procedure has worked in many foreign nations, and in various of our states. It is infinitely better than election in the House under present rules, somewhat better than election in the House and Senate combined under the proposed new rule. Run-off elections have one serious drawback which I have observed in Louisiana. When Candidates A, B, C, and D finish in that order, with A having a substantial lead but not quite enough votes to provide the majority required for election, a run-off is held between Candidates A and B. Now, one might suppose that A, having had a big lead and having been close to election, would win easily; but that is not the case. The cantankerous nature of human beings induces all who voted for B, C, and D to gang up on the leader, so that the better man is defeated and B, a second choice all the way, emerges victor. In 1968 Governor Wallace could still have thrown his support to one of the major candidates in a run-off election and have determined the outcome, but with this significant difference: he would have had to do so in public with the final determination being made at the polls, where all would have had a fair chance to circumvent him. Furthermore, if Wallace voters plus those from one of the major parties proved that they constituted a majority of the nation, publicly arrived at, they would have had not only the right to govern, but also the obligation.

With these two reasonable alternatives available, I can see no reason why the present dangerous system should be extended. This change, too, we should be able to complete in time for the 1972 election.

Step III. We must encourage Congress to give immediate consideration to the four proposed plans for changing our total Presidential election system. Hearings should continue until it is possible to offer the people one amendment which would abolish all parts of the old system and initiate a new.

Obviously, if we could accomplish this quickly, it would make Steps I and II unnecessary, for it would absorb them and automatically put them into operation.

Whether an amendment of such far-reaching purpose could be activated in time to govern the 1972 election is debatable, but if we want the change even as late as 1976 or 1980, we must start now. Committees should be formed across the nation, pressing for an inclusive amendment, and Congress should be reminded at every session that action is obligatory. If immediate results are impossible, and if stop-gap amendments have to be accepted so as to achieve Steps I and II, this should not be allowed to serve as an excuse for halting action on Step III, which must remain our ultimate goal.

Whether or not we can put into operation the three steps I have proposed will depend upon the degree of apathy that will quickly settle upon us, now that we have escaped a situation that might have ended disastrously. No sinner forgets his vows of repentance so quickly as one whose fortunes have made a dramatic improvement.

Also, historical reasons for avoiding reform will again come into play to block any efforts at changing the present system. Smaller states have long believed that since they were assured more electoral votes than their population warranted, they were the gainers from the present system, and for this reason have blocked reform. At first glance they appear to be right. Consider, for example, the 1968 population of the following states, each of which has three electoral votes:

State	Population	Electoral Vote
Alaska	277,000	3
Nevada	453,000	3
Wyoming	315,000	3
Vermont	422,000	3
Delaware	534,000	3
Total	**2,001,000**	**15**

A larger state like Colorado, with about the same total population as the five states combined, gets not 15 electoral votes but 6. And a state like Massachusetts, which has almost three times the population of the five small states combined, receives not three times as many electoral votes, which would be 45, but only 14.

You can appreciate why the smaller states, looking at these figures, prefer to keep the system as it is. But they have read the figures wrong. For many years political experts have suspected that these extra votes which small states receive are illusory, but the mathematical equations to prove this suspicion have been too involved to solve. Nevertheless, Presidential candidates have intuitively known that to win they had to carry the big states. Many believe that Richard Nixon lost the 1960 election because he was sidetracked into fighting for Alaska's 3 votes instead of battling for New York, which then had 45.

I first became interested in this abstract problem of how apparently equal votes actually varied in weight and leverage, because of something that was happening in my home county, which was divided into a large northern area of relatively sparsely settled Republicans and a small southern area of densely concentrated Democrats. In any unprejudiced system of apportionment the five seats to which we were entitled in the state House of Representatives would have been divided about three Republicans in the northern end to two Democrats in the southern, and this would have been the result had the county been divided into five equal districts, each electing one representative. But the Republicans in control of apportionment saw a way to engineer an adroit but perfectly legal gerrymander, and this they did. In the southern end of the county they inscribed one district so that it contained an overwhelming preponderance of Democratic voters. Now, if on the borders of this first district they had carved a second of like dimension, it would have been a swing district, inclining toward the Democratic column; but the canny Republicans did not do this. They lumped the remaining four districts of our county together into one superdistrict, from which they elected four representatives-at-large. Thus our county, instead of returning three Republicans and two Democrats as registrations would have warranted, now elected four Republicans and one Democrat.

At first sight there is nothing much wrong with this. State and federal law alike permitted such gerrymanders at that time, and this one was not particularly offensive, except that many good Democratic votes were effectively submerged in a sea of Republicanism.

I must report that as a Democrat thus submerged, I did not complain, for we play rough politics in Pennsylvania and I felt that if the Republicans were smart enough to devise such a scheme, they were entitled to profit from it. I felt so for two reasons. First, the gerrymander was legal; and second, I looked forward to that day when we Democrats took control of apportionment, for then we intended to throw all the Republicans into two separate and segregated districts in the northern end of the county and to elect three representatives-at-large from an undivided district in the southern end, where the Democrats would predominate. By this trick alone we would switch the county from four Republicans and one Democrat to a more palatable three Democrats and two Republicans. I hoped the Republicans would not protest this legal maneuver, since they had raped us for so many decades.

But the more I studied the problem the more I began to suspect that the real injustice in this situation lay not in party battles between Republicans and Democrats, which my side happened to be losing at the moment, but in the larger moral issue arising from the fact that theoretically equal citizens in my county were in practice very unequal indeed. And the crux of the matter was that the Democrats in the single district, even though each had one vote, were sorely underrepresented as compared to the Republicans in the large district from which four representatives were chosen. I was not able to prove my point mathematically, for as I have said, the formulae were too complicated to be solved at that time, but this did not prevent me from concluding that a grave inequity was being perpetrated.

Consider the figures:

One one-member district	50,000 population
One four-member district	200,000 population

At first glance it would seem that no injustice was involved. But consider a close election, say one in which in each district only a hundred votes separated the two parties. How these final 100 votes were applied in the one-member district would determine one vote in the house; but how the final 100 votes were applied in the four-man constituency would determine four votes in the house. And when the election was over, each citizen among the 50,000 in the first district would be able to bring pressure to bear on his one house member, while each citizen in the larger district had four members whom he might influence.

Recent Supreme Court decisions have, of course, made it possible for citizens to challenge such inequities, and in my county, at least, they have been stopped, for now we elect all our representatives from single-member districts, it having been held that a state could elect all its representatives from multiple-member districts if it wished, but that it could not pick and choose districts for such treatment; and certainly it could not split a single county into some single-member districts and other multiple-member districts, for even though mathematical proof of the injustice of this discrimination was not yet at hand, the suspicion persisted that large blocs of votes carried with them large advantages.

At about the time I was pondering these problems, John F. Banzhaf III, a politically-minded lawyer, had begun working on them with a staff of mathematicians backed up by a battery of computers, and they were able to state and solve the intricate equations which demonstrated the amount of discrimination built into our system and whom it discriminated against. Banzhaf began his analysis with a simplified example:

> Consider the election of a congressman from a single electoral district. Every voter has 1 vote and, therefore, has equal voting power in this election. Suppose, however, that 3 voters, *A, B,* and *C,* were for some reason required to vote as a group and that a bloc of 3 votes would be cast in accordance with the majority vote of *A, B,* and *C.* There are 8 different voting combinations in which *A, B,* and *C* may cast their votes. In 4 of these *A* can alter the way in which the bloc of 3 votes will be cast by changing his own vote. The situation is the same for *B* and for *C;* each can change the outcome in half of the total number of combinations. Thus, each of the three can, by

changing his own vote, affect the way in which the bloc of 3 votes will be cast in 50% of the cases. In contrast, any single elector in the district has 100% control over how his smaller "bloc" of 1 vote should be cast. Since the bloc of 3 votes is three times as effective from the point of view of affecting the election as any single vote, and since A can affect the way in which the bloc of 3 votes will be cast in 50% of the cases, A has more voting power than other voters who have only 100% control over 1 vote; *i.e.,* 50% of 3 votes is greater than 100% of 1 vote. The voting power of A, B, and C has been increased by requiring them to cast their votes as a bloc. Bloc or unit-voting can, therefore, be identified as the crucial factor resulting in the disparities in voting power under the present system [*i.e.,* voting for President by states on a winner-take-all basis].

Progressing to ever larger total groups of voters and to correspondingly larger blocs within those groups, Banzhaf proved that "the voting power of an individual voter increases as the size of his voting group increases," and that in general "the voting power is proportional to the square root of the group's population." He then proceeded to the heart of the matter with this analysis:

As an example of the operation of these principles in their application to the Electoral College, consider the states of New York and Alaska. New York has approximately seventy-four times the population of Alaska. One might suppose that a citizen of New York would have one-seventy-fourth the chance of affecting New York's 43 electoral votes as a voter in Alaska would have of affecting Alaska's 3 votes. However, as has been shown, the relative effectiveness of the two voters depends instead on the ratio of the square roots of the populations, and, therefore, a New Yorker has about one-ninth as much chance of affecting his state's electoral votes as a voter in Alaska has of affecting his. But, because a New Yorker may potentially affect 43 votes as compared with the Alaskan's potential effect on only 3 votes, the New Yorker's decrease in effectiveness with respect to his state's electoral votes is far outweighed by the vastly larger number of electoral votes he may potentially affect. Actually, a New Yorker has almost twice the potential for affecting the overall election as does an

Alaskan voting on the same day in the same election (3.312 compared with 1.838).

The gross inequities of our present system are summarized in Appendix C, Table 1, where it can be seen that in the winner-take-all system, it is the big states like New York, California, Pennsylvania, Ohio, Illinois, and Texas that profit, while smaller states like Maine, New Mexico, Nebraska and Utah suffer. Thus the very states which have emotionally resisted reform have been the heavy losers under the system they were defending.*

Table 2 shows that it is the proportional plan which produces the largest discrepancies between small states and large. If you take California as a base of 1.000, Alaska has 5.212 times the leverage and Nevada 4.132 times. This really sizable imbalance arises from the fact that whereas the state's votes are distributed proportionally, and thus more justly as within the state, the small states have those extra electoral votes for their senators, regardless of size, which produces for them an unjustified power.

Table 3 of the Banzhaf study proves that the district plan produces a much narrower spread of differences than the plan we are now using, but with the relative relationships reversed. Now it is small-population states like Alaska, Nevada, Wyoming, Vermont, and Delaware that prosper, while large-population states like New York, California, Pennsylvania, and Texas are sharply penalized, which explains why the district plan has been called a boon for rural areas and a defeat for urban.

Table 4 proves rather graphically that all these imbalances and leverages disappear when you switch to a direct popular vote. If Alaska has 277,000 people, of whom 82,975 voted for the three principal candidates in 1968, they would have the precise leverage provided by that number of votes and no more. They are thus in an equal position of proportional influence with all the other forty-nine states, and none has a just complaint that he is being penalized or his neighbor rewarded.†

---

*Confining themselves to a more limited problem, Irving Mann and L. S. Shapley of the RAND Corporation concluded that the distribution of power in the present electoral system roughly coincides with the population power of the state and that therefore no state or region is discriminated against. *Values of Large Games, VI. Evaluating the Electoral College Exactly.* RAND Corporation, May, 1962.

†In correspondence with the writer, Mr. Banzhaf pointed out that the problem of my home county, which had stumped me, was relatively simple. If you have a one-member district of 50,000 population contrasted to a four-member district of 200,000 population, with all members voting independently of each other, the weighted advan-

With these facts in mind, we are prepared to look at the four proposed reforms to see how each would affect the regions of our country, the elements of our population, and the fortunes of our political parties, for as Senator Bayh has correctly pointed out, "Electoral systems are rarely, if ever, neutral. The present electoral voting system is no exception." First I must discuss the political elements common to all four, after which I will try to pinpoint where these four proposals stray from neutrality.

The Electoral College. The complete vacuity of this College is proved by the fact that it provides no advantage to either party, nor to any segment of the society, nor to the nation as a whole. Since it is an excrescence it could be abolished without harm to anyone. If it operated today in its original conception of learned citizens of prominence meeting to select a leader, it would probably favor Republicans in placid times, since Republicans would appeal to the solid reputations of the electors, who would be men of similar character, and the Democrats in time of trouble, since then the electors would, being men of good sense, be prepared to espouse new or even radical reforms. At times in the fall of 1968 I occasionally felt that in a radical and undefined situation such as the one we might have faced, the inherent discipline of the Republican party might have given it an advantage in a chaotic Electoral College; ostracism from the Union League Club, the country club, the bankers association, and the channels of suburban society would have been a much more severe penalty to the straying Republican than any ostracism I could have suffered, simply because like many Democrats I belonged to little from which I could have been ostracized.

The electoral system. At the moment one accepts an electoral system in which each state is given so many votes to dispose of as it wishes, one introduces two basic inequalities from which he never recovers. First, the award of two votes for the state's two senators, regardless of population, establishes a small bias in favor of the small states (if one takes into account election by the House). Second, whenever a state's total number of votes is cast as a bloc, the state with the larger number of votes to manipulate will be at an advantage, and this has to create a large bias in favor of the large states. Furthermore, when the winner-take-all system becomes a tradition across the country, this inherent bias is enshrined and inescapable. I

tage of a voter in the four-member constituency is approximately 2.000 times (twice) that of his neighbor who votes for only one member.

will defer an analysis of who wins and loses by this system until the next paragraph.

The winner-take-all system of allocating a state's electoral votes. This arbitrary system which grew up by custom and is not sanctioned by the Constitution provides substantial advantage to large states, to minorities who through concentrated voting can swing those large states, and to the states who restrict their suffrage, in that it doesn't matter how many citizens vote, so long as a plurality of one Republican or one Democrat or one Wallace supporter votes; the state's entire electoral vote goes the way that one man decided and the state gains no advantage from getting out a large vote. Because of a whole constellation of factors this system probably favors the Democrats, although this advantage is offset by a collateral component of the system, which is considered next.

Choosing a President in the House. Here the smaller states have an enormous advantage, so vast that I have not seen numerical evaluations of it. The inherent discrepancies were illustrated on page 26, where the comparison of Alaska with California was made. The system favors small states, rural areas as opposed to urban, conservatives rather than liberals, majority population groups rather than minorities, and Republicans rather than Democrats, but only slightly. It is, however, a part of the basic compromise on which our nation was founded and none of the imbalances I point out were accidental or unforeseen.

Nationwide primaries. These would represent a considerable advantage to smaller states, and a corresponding loss to large ones, in that a party could risk running a man from a state of any size rather than concentrating on candidates from large states in hopes of picking up their big blocs of votes. The publicity advantage now enjoyed by states like New Hampshire and Oregon, who run notorious but rarely definitive primaries, would be lost. I suspect that one party or the other would gain some advantage from nationwide primaries, but I cannot detect what it would be.

Our present plan. Considering all the elements that govern elections today, this plan favors large states, cities, small voting blocs if they unite to control a city or a state, and any aggressive minority like Puerto Ricans or bankers which can goad its members to an unusual attendance at the polls. As President Kennedy cleverly detected, it probably favors Democrats slightly, except that if an election is thrown into the House, Republicans are slightly favored, as we have seen, and the smaller states enormously so.

Now we can consider the four proposed plans.

The automatic plan. Insofar as opportunity for leverage is concerned, this plan is identical with the present one. As I have shown, abolishing the Electoral College does not affect any balances of power. However, if the recent improvements to this plan are adopted, and they should be, whereby inconclusive elections would no longer be thrown into the House but decided by a run-off election, then the considerable advantages which accrue to small states in House elections would be lost.

The district plan. As the Banzhaf studies show, this is the most equitable plan if the electoral system is retained. It does nevertheless reverse the slight Democratic advantage of the present system into an equally slight advantage for the Republicans, but in my opinion neither of these advantages is of a magnitude that would justify apprehension, and decisions must not be reached with them as a prime consideration. It also reverses the relative advantages of rural and urban areas, augmenting the former and diminishing the latter. This plan would diminish the power of large states and convey that advantage to the small. If it had been in operation in the 1960 election it would have produced an outright victory for Nixon of 278–245 instead of the Kennedy victory of 303–219, but that was an unusual election and other proposed reforms would, had they been operating, also have produced a Nixon victory. In the past, this plan would have elected Andrew Jackson in 1824 instead of John Quincy Adams; and Grover Cleveland in 1888 instead of Benjamin Harrison. The results cannot be accurately ascertained at this time, but the plan would probably have resulted in a victory for Stephen Douglas over Abraham Lincoln in 1860; and for Charles E. Hughes over Woodrow Wilson in 1916.

The proportional plan. Because it is linked to the electoral system, this plan would transfer considerable power to our smaller states, at the expense of our larger. Had this plan been operating in the 1960 election, it would have produced a Nixon victory by one-half vote: Nixon 266.075, Kennedy 265.623, others 5.302. (A later study reported by the Library of Congress Legislative Reference Service shows Nixon 266.136, Kennedy 263.662, others 7.202. Differences between the two results stem from the manner in which the contested votes from Alabama are applied.) But there seems to be no permanent advantage to either party, unless the leverage of the cities were so sharply curtailed as to damage the Democrats. Historically, this plan would have elected the Democrat Winfield S. Hancock in 1880 instead of James A. Garfield, even though the latter had won the popular vote; and in 1896 it would have made the Democrat William Jennings Bryan President instead of William McKinley.

Direct popular vote. As we have seen, this would equalize state advantages, but it would still enable cities, by virtue of their concentrations of population, to exercise their old leverage. It would abolish the present power of minority groups to influence large blocs of electoral votes, but any minority or group which could muster an exceptional turnout at the polls would have an advantage. Because electioneering would have to be done largely by television, this plan might seem to favor the Republicans, who could buy more television time, but it is the person who might vote Democratic who could more easily be swayed to vote by a dazzling performance of a Democratic candidate. Also, since there would be an extra incentive to vote, the larger turnouts that might result could favor the Democrats.

What all this speculation adds up to is the fact that the process of electing a President is a very tricky operation, whatever process is used. The present system has evolved over many years and has achieved a balance which works; any modification will hurt some and help others, but the correction of obvious weaknesses will help us all.

In the forthcoming debate over what corrections to make, I think those concerned should state where they stand. I am obviously in favor of abolishing the Electoral College immediately. It must not be allowed to meet even one more time. The process leading to a constitutional amendment which would eliminate at least this error must be started immediately, even though the resulting amendment might have to be superseded later when more fundamental changes became possible. All plans which have been advanced for keeping the College, but with restraints and protections, seem inherently dangerous to me and I could accept none; as long as the College existed, clever ways would be found to manipulate it. It should be given no extension of life. It should be abolished now.

I also believe that throwing inconclusive elections into the House must be stopped, and I would hope that this could be accomplished in the amendment ending the Electoral College. Substituting election by the joint House and Senate is an improvement, but even this is so

open to manipulation, pressure, and fraud that I would find it difficult to sponsor such a plan. I much prefer the run-off election as
being quick, efficient, and decisive. It is also the best method for in-
suring a visible legitimacy.

As to the four alternative plans, I must choose in obedience to
what I have learned in politics. I have already spoken of my philosophical apprenticeship to John C. Calhoun; my practical training
came at the hands of an unknown Irishman on Espiritu Santo, the
savage island south of Guadalcanal.

In the early autumn of 1944 the Navy commander of Espiritu
Santo received a directive from President Roosevelt's office in Washington ordering him, and all other island commanders, to ensure that
a proper election was held in their areas. There were to be no slip-ups
or errors. The commander looked down his roster of officers and saw
that I had taught history, so he summoned me and growled, "You are
the election officer of this island, and there are to be no slip-ups or
errors. If there are, it's your neck."

I proceeded to organize the snappiest Presidential election the island of Espiritu Santo had ever seen. I enlisted the aid of some men
who had been commercial artists in private life and we plastered the
island with reminders that "Your Vote Is Your Freedom. Use It."
"Pick the Best Man and Back Him. Vote." We also had one for which
I was directly responsible: "Don't Be Dumb. Vote."

I next set up a system whereby every man, as he entered and left
chow line, was reminded that by going to the proper building he
could vote. We sent speakers who delivered one-minute addresses before the movies started, and if there was anyone on the island, including the natives, who remained ignorant of the Roosevelt-Dewey
election under way back home, it wasn't my fault.

The island commander and I were not disturbed when we received notice that a personal representative of the President would
visit the island to check on our preparations for the election. Special
inspection was to be made to be sure that Governor Dewey was getting a fair shake, and on this point I had been meticulous. I doubted
if any other island in the Pacific could show a better election than the
one we were running.

When the courier plane landed and the ramp came down, we saw
a red-faced Irishman in a sweaty blue civilian suit descend. The first
thing he saw was a huge sign which said, "Vote. That's What We're
Fighting For." When he looked beyond that he saw other signs, and

when he came face to face with me he saw that I wore a large hand-made button which said, "Vote!"

The red in his face turned to purple. He studied the various signs and exploded, "What in hell is going on here?"

The island commander, a notoriously nervous type, began to sweat and asked what was wrong, and the visitor bellowed, "Wrong! Everything's wrong!"

The commander grabbed for me and shoved me forward. "This officer is in charge."

The Irishman looked at me compassionately and asked in a voice dripping with frustration, "Son, what in hell do you think you're doing?"

"I'm getting out the vote," I said.

"We want everyone to have the right to vote," he explained slowly. "We don't want them to vote."

He surveyed the airport and said, "Somebody has done a lot of work here. I can see that. But it's all been wrong. So you get your crew together and take down every damned sign on this island. By nightfall I don't want to see a single election sign . . . not anywhere! And when you've given that order, I want to see you in the commander's office."

I assembled my crew and told them the news. "Everything down." I began by ripping down a sign that one of my men had carefully painted.

"What's going on?" he asked.

"Don't ask me, I'm totally confused."

When the wrecking crews were on their way I reported to the Irishman, who now had a glass of whiskey and a fresh shirt. He was an amiable man, a wonderful politician of the Boston school, and in later years I tried to find his name, because I supposed that he was operating as a member of John F. Kennedy's Irish mafia. He had a most practical sense of politics, and the four or five hours I spent with him formed an unforgettable part of my education.

"The Navy has one objective only," he explained, "and keep it always in mind. We would be happy if every sailor on this island and every sailor on every ship around this island failed to vote. But we must have a careful written record proving that the Navy gave him the privilege of voting . . . had he so desired.

"Let me put it another way. Our sole objective is to prevent senators from getting letters like this one . . . six months after the election." He showed me a letter to a New England senator in which an enlisted man had complained about the 1942 election: "I would of voted for you, Senator, but the damned Navy wouldn't let me."

"We tracked that case down, and of course the Navy had allowed the kid to vote, and thank God we had a signed paper to prove it. The kid had never bothered to write for a ballot. And we had a paper to prove that, too. Michener, we want to have a paper proving that every lousy human being on this island had a right to vote. But we sure as hell don't want them to exercise it."

In expansive detail he explained his theories, happy to have as an audience someone who could understand what he was talking about. "You do not further democracy," he argued, "by encouraging a whole lot of people to vote. This country is kept alive by a small nucleus of devoted Republicans and Democrats who think enough of it to work their damned shoes to the pavement and their suits to a frazzle doing the job that others wouldn't touch. They keep the parties together. They run the Congress and the states and the cities. They work at registration, at the polls, at the primaries, at God knows what else. They should do the voting and not someone who wakes up to politics one day every four years.

"I would be quite happy if about ten per cent of those eligible to vote did so. We'd have better government because they'd know what they were voting about. You see many stories about the low voting percentage in Mississippi. There's nothing wrong with that. It isn't the low percentage that's wrong, of itself, but the manner in which the percentage is kept low. They won't let Negroes vote and they should. But if they did, only a few would vote. They'd be the good ones, and their opinion would be valuable. As for the others, they're no better than the Irish in Boston.

"You take this Boston congressman that I helped send to Washington. Very smart fellow. I was in his office one day when a deputation of nineteen workingmen from his district came down to raise hell about the way he'd voted on a labor bill. They swore they'd run him out of office at the next election. He was very contemptuous of them and practically told them to get out of his office. When they were gone I told him if he kept up like that he'd lose for sure next time, and he told me, 'They said they'd vote me out of office. How many of those lunkers do you think are registered? When I heard they were coming down I looked it up.' He buzzed for his girl and she gave him the figures. Of the nineteen who took the trouble to come to

Washington, four were registered. He said, 'This afternoon I'll write each of those four a real swell letter . . . embossed letterhead . . . everything . . . and I'll keep them in line. The other fifteen? You know where they'll be on election day? Home drinking beer.'"

He was intensely interested in politics and seemed to me to be saying that the old Greek attitude toward democracy was the only one that made sense. I asked him if he held the general public in contempt. "Not at all! We have the best public in the world and they deserve good government. But the vote should be kept difficult. Let every man in the nation who really wants to vote do so, but don't make it easy for him. Make it very tough and you'll weed out the automatic voters who never know what it's all about and merely mark the ballot.

"One thing we've got to change. This absentee ballot business. Stop all absentee ballots. The only man entitled to vote is someone who has followed the course of the entire election so he knows what's going on. And to do this he has to be on the scene. One radio speech can disclose a candidate's weakness or strike a spark of humanity. You have to be on the scene to catch this, and if you don't react to it you're not entitled to vote.

"Besides," he said sardonically, "about eighty per cent of absentee ballots vote for your man anyway"—in those days I was Republican—"and it's not fair to give Dewey all those ready-made votes."

He talked on and on, sharing secrets of Boston politics, and finally I asked, "Would you restrict the ballot?"

"Never!" he shouted. "I'd make it as liberal as possible. Every Negro should have the right to vote, every working-man. I'd even drop the voting age to eighteen. I want the help of every good man in the nation. But I'd make it very difficult to vote. I'd want a man to have to take conscious effort to register, to vote in the primaries and to vote in the general." In some disgust he took from his briefcase a sample ballot for the state of Massachusetts and spread it on the table between us. Contemptuously he went from one contest to another, excoriating now Republicans, now Democrats. "How can a man on this island possibly know what the values are in this election back home? Take these two clowns. How can he decide which is worse than the other? Under no circumstances should a man on this island be permitted to vote in this election. And I don't want them voting . . . unless they come to you with their tongues hanging out begging for a ballot. And then they ought to vote for only the top spot . . . Roosevelt or Dewey . . . because about the rest they can understand nothing."

He concluded with a statement I have never forgotten. "I believe totally in democracy but I want to see great crowds at the polls in only one condition. When they are filled with blind fury at the mismanagement of the country and are determined to throw the bastards out. From time to time votes like that are necessary to keep the system clean. For the rest of the time I think you leave politics to those of us who really care."

Then, to prove that he was a politician, he asked quietly, "Would it help you with the commanding officer if I told him that . . . except for the signs . . . you had done a splendid job on this island?" I said it would.

As election officer for Espiritu Santo, I posted no more exhortations, made no more speeches, but on our election day, which came in mid-October, I think that every man on the island who really wanted to vote for either Roosevelt or Dewey did so. We made it difficult for them to find the voting booths, but they found them.

With this background I have reached certain conclusions about what we should do after we have abolished the Electoral College and House elections. I am not in favor of a direct popular vote for President. I fear that such a vote would be vulnerable to demagoguery, to wild fluctuations of public reaction, to hysteria generated by television, and to the tearing down of the old safeguards which have protected the various regions of our nation. A direct vote would hand too much leverage to the cities, and in spite of claims that it would be easy to administer, I judge that it would be rather difficult because of absentee ballots, the temptation to trickery, and the tremendous pressures that would be placed upon certifying officials. Today, if the officials of State X run a crooked election, it affects the electoral vote of that state but can be otherwise quarantined. If State X's corrupt votes were tossed into the general balloting, they might corrupt the entire procedure and bring our whole election system into discredit. Far from enhancing the legitimacy of the outcome, this would cast shadows upon it.

I am opposed to direct voting for another reason. I think there is much good in the electoral system. I prefer voting by states and allowing regions to exercise advantages which mere numbers would not give them. I hold this to be a part of the American genius, an invention which has helped hold us together when others have flown apart in sectionalism. The fact that direct voting would abolish this old tradition lessens the attractiveness of the new plan for me. Nor would it be as efficient as some claim. Senator Mundt is exaggerating, but not much, when he claims, "If the direct popular vote had been in operation in the 1968 election, we would not have known until late November who was going to be our next President, because of absentee ballots and the slowness of counting. The trading and pulling and uncertainty might have been with us until mid-December."

Having made these objections, I must now confess that even though direct popular voting is not my first choice, I see much merit in the plan; and since it seems to be the choice of the vast majority of the American public, if the polls are to be believed, and since its sponsors are among the finest political minds of this nation, I am conceding no principle when I say that if I cannot get the plan I want, I will want the one I can get. And certainly, if we had the option of either keeping our present plan with all its defects or adopting the new plan of direct voting, I would not hesitate a moment to opt for the latter. The technical imperfections of direct popular voting could be cleared up in time, I suppose, and as for the philosophical objection that the people might run wild at moments of hysteria, I would rather risk that inevitable concomitant of democracy than to surrender democracy itself.

Direct popular voting is, therefore, my second choice, and I would not lament if circumstances made it my first. I would be willing to work very hard to attain an amendment for such a vote, for this plan holds far more promise than it does danger.

The proportional plan seems to me an attack on the historic rights of states and regions. It not only reverses the present discrepancies but also magnifies them without offering just compensation in the way of increased effectiveness. Most serious is the likelihood that this plan would encourage the growth of numerous minority parties, and to this I am strongly opposed, due to my long experience in foreign nations which suffer from such proliferation. If Israel ultimately collapses, it will not be because of Arab pressure from the outside, but because she fosters such a bewildering number of contending parties within. The delays that would be involved in determining who had won an election would be both dangerous and frustrating. Senator Mundt's strictures against the delay inherent in the direct popular vote would apply with even more relevancy here. When the total machinery, because of its use of three decimal places, depends upon an absolutely accurate vote, how could we expect such a vote to be forthcoming quickly? I have not yet seen the proportional computations for the 1968 election, but they could not have been known with accuracy much before the second week in December, which was the earliest I was able to obtain final election figures from the fifty states. (The figures were released on December 13, 1968, but could, I suppose, have been speeded up had an election depended upon them. Also, I realize that by the time 90 per cent of the vote was in, clear patterns would have developed, but I also remember that in 1960 the proportional plan could not have produced a final result till well into December.)

I am afraid that proportionalism is an alluring concept for college sophomores, for it does speak to justice, equality, encouragement to minority groups, and many other laudable aims, but in a complex democracy like ours it does not seem to work, and the benefits which derive from it are more than offset by the disadvantages. I cannot imagine myself supporting an amendment which would introduce proportional voting, at least not until the many drawbacks which I see today had been eliminated. Having said this, I acknowledge that this plan would eliminate the Electoral College and the House election, two desirable accomplishments.

The district plan has much to commend it. It preserves many of the traditional balances of our nation and does not impose severe disadvantages on any type of state. The small swing in favor of the Republicans merely corrects an imbalance that has long operated in a contrary direction and does not alarm me. The switch from urban advantage to rural does. I am suspicious of any change like that at this time, for it seems to me to fly into the face of contemporary history and therefore to be a real step backward, not toward sensible conservatism but toward a panic flight from reality. The real drawback to this plan, however, is the list of sponsors; one might say that if these gentlemen are for a bill, the rest of us ought to be against it. I do not feel that way. It appears to me that these hard-shell conservatives realize that change is inevitable and prefer to see it move somewhat in their direction rather than toward a direct popular vote, which to them smacks of too much democracy. They may be right. At any rate, I would by no means dismiss their proposal and would indeed work for it if my first two preferences were proved impractical of attainment. However, before I supported the plan its sponsors would have to correct two errors that at present disqualify it. On page 69 I said that if any proposed plan fails to abolish both the College and the House election, "it should be discarded at once." The present proposal keeps these two anachronisms but hedges them about with just enough safeguards so that many voters would be reassured. I would not. On pages 102–103 I have explained why I could sponsor neither. Therefore, this proposal would have to jettison the Electoral College and House-Senate election before I could sponsor it. If John C. Calhoun were alive today, I suppose he would support this plan as it is, and there I would part company with him.

By elimination, then, I find myself supporting the automatic plan as revised. In essence this is the electoral plan we now have, minus the College, which is abolished, with election permitted at 40 per cent of the electoral vote, and with a run-off election if no candidate wins that percentage. Its unchanged features have been historically proven. It is about as close to a true democracy as we shall get, or ought to get, and it is just. I prefer having the states retain their electoral votes, even though imbalances occur among them, and in spite of Senator Smith's ridicule, I like the fact that this electoral vote magnifies the margins of victory. It is good, I think, that the Presidential election, which might degenerate into a vast national brawl, is broken into segments of manageable size. I am by strong persuasion a Democrat, but I have never believed in a raw democracy of merely adding up total votes. I believe in a system whereby we elect officials, such as senators and representatives, to whom we delegate the responsibility of governing for us; by extension I favor a system of selecting our President whereby each state has its own leverage and in which the two major political parties play a significant role.

I have considered carefully two weaknesses in the automatic plan. First, election by only 40 per cent of the electoral vote is vastly different from election by 40 per cent of the popular vote and introduces factors which I am not able at this time to assess. Permitting a candidate to become President when he has won less than a majority of the popular vote has become so common in our political life that it is an established tradition, and an accepted one. I have already shown that five times in this century, from Wilson to Nixon, men have been so elected; in the preceding century the same thing happened ten times: J. Q. Adams, Polk, Taylor, Buchanan, Lincoln 1860, Hayes, Garfield, Cleveland, Harrison, Cleveland. I do not see how anyone could complain of a tradition which has worked so well.

But when we allow a man to win with only 40 per cent of the electoral vote we are establishing a procedure, considering the way in which the electoral vote magnifies slight differences in the popular vote, whereby a man could win the Presidency with a marked minority of the popular vote while his opponent was losing in spite of a conspicuous majority. (A brief study of the states, their population and their electoral votes, will show how this could be done.) I consider this innovation an error and would oppose it. A run-off election should be held whenever no candidate wins an outright majority of the electoral vote. If we are going to improve the system, let us abolish the possibility of having Presidents forced upon us who have not won at least 50 per cent of the electoral vote.

The second objection is that by amendment this plan would freeze into the Constitution the present winner-take-all tradition of allocating electoral votes, whereas now it stands as a tradition only and could be changed by action of the states without an amendment. I find this objection irrelevant, because the states are not going to change and because the tradition is so firmly rooted and has proved so workable that it is already, for practical purposes, as secure as if it were a part of the Constitution. Making it so alters nothing.

To summarize, I prefer the automatic plan and will work hard for its adoption. If it is found to have little chance in view of the groundswell of support for direct popular election, I would be able to work in good faith for that solution.

As to the two proposed general improvements, I am not in favor of a national primary because I believe it would diminish the power and vitality of our political parties, and that could not be constructive. I do wish we could choose our Vice-President in some better way, but I do not know how, and if no workable plan is forthcoming, I would find myself grudgingly accepting a national primary to attain that goal. I am repelled by the idea of having one man, in the heat of a convention victory, deciding for us who our next Vice-President and possibly President is to be. I realize that Section 2 of the Twenty-fifth Amendment empowers the President to nominate, by himself, a new Vice-President whenever there is a vacancy in that office, which seems to be a continuation into the White House of the bad old practice of the convention, but there is a significant difference. When the President-nominate at the convention hand-picks his man, his act requires only the confirmation of the convention, which is given automatically by the very men who have just nominated him.

Under Amendment Twenty-five, when, as elected President, he does the same thing, his act must be confirmed by a majority vote of both houses of Congress. I judge this to be an excellent rule, for I cannot imagine in recent years a supine House and Senate accepting a second-class nominee; today, when at least one of the bodies is often in the hands of the opposition party, there would be little likelihood of confirmation unless the man chosen were of demonstrated merit. We must devise some system of similar probity for the selection of Vice-Presidents at our conventions.

Recently Roscoe Drummond has proposed that a nationwide primary be held, but that it be advisory only. I see much merit in this. Its advantages would be twofold, in that it would preserve the function of the party, whose responsibility would continue for actually nominating the candidate; and since the primaries we already have are merely advisory, Drummond's plan would merely broaden the base so that instead of being unduly influenced by New Hampshire, with a population of only 702,000, we would be listening to the advice of the whole nation, with a population of more than 200,000,000. I would support this plan and would hope that we might establish a tradition whereby Vice-Presidents had to be chosen from among the men who stood well in the national primary.

When I state that I prefer the national convention to the national primary, I certainly do not refer to the two conventions held in 1968, for these were so disgraceful that they harmed politics and damaged our national self-respect. The Republican gaucheries at Miami were unbelievable in a year of war abroad, civil strife at home, problems engulfing our cities, and profound experiments under way in space. None of these vital issues were reflected in the convention; instead we had those awful balloons, those tedious nominating speeches for nobodies from Alaska and Hawaii, those repulsive spontaneous demonstrations, the scenes of calloused jockeying back and forth over trivialities, the accidental glimpse of discredited old men trying their best to dictate whom the Vice-Presidential nomination should go to. Only the even worse disgrace of the Democrats at Chicago erased the nineteenth-century sideshow the Republicans engineered. Most of the people I know under thirty dismissed the whole procedure as beneath their contempt. One clever chap confided to me, "You miss the whole point. It's a very deft device of the Republicans. They're making their show so bad that all young people will be infuriated and unable to tolerate more of the same at Chicago."

As for what the Democrats accomplished in that city, I can speak only with awe. In four days they converted certain victory into defeat, with superannuated bosses from a bygone age cavorting on television, with police revoking every ideal being mouthed on the platform, and with insolence of office replacing exchange of ideas. It left me ashamed and prepared for defeat; in time my own sense of history erased the former, and my dedication to a good fight made me do what I could to avoid the defeat; but I can say that in spite of that dedication this convention nearly finished me in politics. Many young people quit entirely, but perhaps we can win them back with the kind of convention I am thinking about.

I know of no one who wants a repetition of either Miami or Chicago, but I do know many who look forward to Republicans and Democrats meeting, each in their own time, to fight the intellectual and tactical battles of national politics, and I am one.

As to the length of the campaign, I realize that common sense dictates a shorter one. If England and France can run successful national elections in a third of the time we take, it can obviously be done; but I find that I have no strong feelings of support for change in our system. When I ran for Congress, I campaigned from February to November, a murderous route, but I learned so much in the process that each day was worth the effort. I look with grave apprehension at a system which would eliminate face-to-face encounters and substitute campaigning by television; I do not want to be governed by men who have appeared only on television, in some insulated studio far from the milling crowds of living human beings, for I know that such men will have missed that vital contact with cantankerous human beings which knocks sense into the politician's skull and humility into his arrogance. I would, therefore, speak neither for nor against shortened campaigns, trusting that whatever the majority decided would probably be right. This leads us then to the last two steps for immediate action:

Step IV. We must all start studying immediately the four proposed plans—automatic, district, proportional, direct—and decide the merits of each, giving our ardent support to that one which will permit us to elect our Presidents honestly, fairly, and simply.

Step V. If it becomes apparent that the plan we prefer is not attainable, then we must quickly throw our support to the one that is, unless it is totally objectionable. When it is decided what constitutional amendment will be offered the people, we must work diligently to see that it is adopted. Write to your congressmen now. Write to your state legislators now.

My own estimates as to timetable are as follows. We ought to be able to formulate, pass in Congress, submit to the states, and pass before 1972 a constitutional amendment abolishing the Electoral College. The chances for this are about 40 per cent in favor, 60 per cent against, but these could be improved by public pressure.

There is a smaller chance that we could produce and pass an amendment abolishing House elections. I would estimate the situation to be about 30 per cent in favor, 70 per cent against, but again, public pressure could improve this.

The likelihood of getting one of the major amendments through Congress within the immediate future is not good. However, if one did get through, I would judge that the states might ratify it rather promptly. In my own mind I am shooting for 1976 or 1980, which would be about the best I could foresee. However, if the groundswell of popular demand continues, and if the polls in 1970 sustain the enthusiasm evident in 1968, there would be a slim chance that something might be accomplished sooner.

Nothing, of course, will be accomplished in any of these areas unless an extraordinary public pressure is maintained, so the determination really rests with the citizens.

A FINAL FANTASY

I have saved till last an aspect of our present system which seems totally bizarre, for I want the reader to savor the stupidity of the system under which he governs himself. My previous arguments have been to reason; this one involves sheer folly.

In the period following the November election I was much amused at editorial writers who congratulated the nation on having escaped the formidable dangers that could have grown out of the Electoral College or a House election. Everyone wrote as if the nation were home safe after a perilous voyage, but I did not share this feeling of assurance.

I was especially apprehensive about those articles which found satisfaction in the collapse of Governor Wallace's effort to steal the election. The authors wrote as if Wallace had been completely defeated and had no more power to do harm; whereas I thought the little judge now posed an even greater threat, though one less likely to materialize.

"Suppose," I asked myself the morning after election as I listened to congratulations over our narrow escape, "that in the interval between now and December 16 Richard Nixon either dies or withdraws. What then?"

I am aware that in his final pre-election speech to the nation Nixon spoke harshly of people who speculate like ghouls on such matters, and I apologize for mentioning this one now; but I am concerned about the liberty of two hundred million people and the destiny of my nation, and it is my duty to contemplate such possibilities, especially since they exercised me much in that critical period.

I am not asking a hypothetical question, nor am I wasting the reader's time with speculation on something that could not happen. Indeed, it has already happened, except that in this instance the man who died was not the winner but the loser. In 1872 Ulysses S. Grant was the nominee for a second term on the Republican ticket and was opposed by Horace Greeley on the Democratic. Grant won a clear victory in the popular vote, a majority of 728,612 out of a total vote of 6,466,138, and this would have produced in the Electoral College a commanding majority of 286–83, except that Greeley's vote was never counted, because on November 29, 1872, two weeks before the College met, Greeley died. Since his death could have no bearing on the Presidential succession, the Democrats did not bother to nominate a substitute. Of those votes which would have gone to Greeley, 63 were scattered arbitrarily, with 3 of the faithful electors still voting for the dead man out of respect and 17 not voting at all. In accurate histories the electoral vote in this election is recorded as 286–0 for a reason which will become apparent in the next paragraph.

When the Electoral College passed its results along to Congress, that body decided that it was preposterous for the electors to have voted for a man who had died before they convened, and Congress refused to record any votes cast on his behalf. And tradition is clear that Congress will not accept electoral votes cast for dead men; they are automatically nullified. I judged, therefore, during those anxious days when I was studying this eventuality, that this precedent would be honored, and that if Richard Nixon were to die in that gray interval, any electoral votes which might be cast for him would be disregarded.

This would mean that unless the Republican party could decide swiftly and securely upon someone to replace Nixon, the election would be inconclusive; it would fail to produce a President and would be thrown into the House. (It is clear that when the Electoral College elects a Vice-President they are doing just that, and only that; the man so designated is Vice-President and remains so until such time as the House indicates that it is unable to settle upon a President, in which contingency the Vice-President serves as President, holding the office only until such time as a President is agreed upon, however tardy the House might be in settling that issue. Upon retiring in favor of the newly designated President, he resumes the Vice-Presidency.)

Had Nixon died, it would have been obligatory for the Republican National Committee to designate some individual to stand for the Presidency and to hope that their nomination would be acceptable to the Republican members of the Electoral College. The nation would then have held its breath to see how the 302 Republican electors who had been pledged to Nixon would react to the new man. If they accepted him, he would be the next President. If they wavered, and if thirty-three defected, the Republicans would not have won and the election would have been thrown into the House, where because of their control of the state delegations, the Democrats would possibly have been able to elect Humphrey.

What are the chances that the Republicans would have been able to nominate a candidate quickly and impose him upon the electors? I trust that the reader will follow my reasoning carefully so as to appreciate what might have happened between November 5 and December 16, 1968.

To begin with, at the moment Nixon's death was announced, the 302 Republican electors pledged to him would have become the most important citizens in the United States, for they alone would have held the fate of the Presidency in their hands, and all decisions made as to a substitute nominee would have had to be made with one question in mind: "Will the electors agree?" It would not have mattered what the Republican National Committee or the general public thought of the new man, but only what this handful of 302 men and women, arbitrarily and capriciously chosen, thought.

Again the forty-five electors pledged to Wallace would have become of crucial importance, because if any of the Republican electors did waver, unable to accept the nominee which the national committee proposed to ram down their throats, the Wallace men could have rushed in to arrange a deal which would either grant or deny victory to the Republicans. Remember that the Republicans would have had to settle this matter in the Electoral College; their prospects would not have been bright in the House, and if to win in the College they required the Wallace votes, the temptation would have been great to arrange a deal for them. Governor Wallace would have been in a better position to exercise leverage than before; and his offer of a covenant, more attractive.

And finally, the 191 Democrats would have found themselves in a position to dictate to the Republicans whom the Republicans should nominate to the vacancy, for these electors were free to swing one way or the other, depending upon what tactical situation developed.

If Nixon's removal had occurred early in this period, there would have been time for the Republican National Committee to reconvene its members in emergency session and to hold, in effect, another complete convention with the same procedures as had operated in Miami earlier in the summer. This convention, by a careful display of honesty and fair play, might have come up with a candidate who would satisfy the electors and enlist their undivided loyalty.

But at the very beginning of the convention the party would have faced a crucial decision. In the normal course of events it would be natural for any party so faced with crisis to elevate the Vice-Presidential candidate to the Presidency and then to select a new Vice-President. But I doubt that in 1968 the Republicans could have promoted their Vice-President to President with any hope of keeping their electors pledged to vote for him when the College convened. The great newspapers of the country, the television commentators, the news magazines, and the general public would all have protested in the name of patriotism and reason and would have applied such tremendous pressure on the Republican electors that some would surely have defected, enough I think to have put Wallace and the Democrats back into a bargaining position. This possibility the Republican leadership would not have risked.

Let us suppose, therefore, that the Republicans would have had to

choose between candidates who had come before the summer convention and that the final choice had been between two men, say
Ronald Reagan of California and Nelson Rockefeller of New York—
two men even farther apart in ideology than in geography—and let
us suppose further that the Rockefeller forces had been able to blast
out a victory. Would the 302 electors have stood firm behind this
choice? I doubt it. Fantastic pressures would have been applied to
every Republican elector, and those whose hearts inclined toward
Reagan, or whose egos had been scarred in the fight, would have been
susceptible to that pressure. I doubt that the Republicans could have
maintained discipline; I doubt that Rockefeller would have been able
to collect the 270 votes required.

At this point the Wallace people would have had every right to try
to put together a coalition behind Reagan or some other attractive
conservative in hopes of drawing to their candidate the support of
Democratic conservatives.

The Democrats, meanwhile, would have been undergoing their
own agony. At first they would have judged rather smugly—and in-
correctly, I think—that if they stood firm they would wind up with a
good chance of throwing the election into the House, where they
could elect Humphrey. But they would soon have awakened to the
fact that it was George Wallace who really held the balance of power,
and whereas he did not like Rockefeller and had spoken disrespect-
fully of him, he liked Humphrey even less and was determined to
deprive him of the Presidency. The Democrats would thus have found
themselves in a position in which the Electoral College vote was
going to be decided without their participation.

In the early days of December rumors would have flooded this
nation; intricate calculations would have been made each hour, and
the threat of what Wallace might do, or the extent to which the Republicans might be indebted to him in case he threw the victory to
them, would so have haunted the Democrats that they would probably have concluded, "It is better for us to make a deal with Nelson
Rockefeller," and I suppose that this would have been proposed by
the party leaders.

I can say this. As I stood on that rostrum on December 16 waiting
for the last elector to sign, I could not state with certainty how even I
would have voted had Nixon died, and I felt fairly certain that few of
the electors before me could have predicted their votes either. There

would have been an insane scramble for votes, and no man can say in retrospect how his character would have reacted to the pressures to which he would have been exposed.

A worse situation could have developed. Had Nixon died late in the interval, the Republicans would not have had time to assemble in formal convention. Hectic telephone and telegraph consultations would have had to suffice. At best the decision would have been peremptory and little calculated to enlist popular or electoral support; at worst it would have appeared as an unwarranted dictatorship which would have repelled certain of the electors. Each tendency which I have noted as potentially disruptive to the 302 electors in case a convention selected the substitute would have been magnified if the candidate had been dictated, and I seriously doubt that the Republicans could have held their electors in line.

In either case, the uncertainty of the last two weeks prior to the convening of the Electoral College would have been extraordinary and the outcome would have been a lottery, predictable by no one.

The point I wish to make is not that the system is complex and open to error; many excellent systems have those defects. The peculiar weakness of this system, and one which totally disqualifies it, is that the vital decisions are made by members of the Electoral College bound by no law, no tradition, no restraint, and little common sense. We place our destiny in the hands of men and women who are not even nominated or elected seriously. It is unfair to both the nation and the electors to impose upon them such obligations and temptations.

In what follows, I have attempted to codify the curious mélange of law and custom that governs the contingencies that might arise during a national election. I think these ought to be kept in mind when one tries to decide what changes we should make in our election system, and I shall divide the summer, fall, and winter of an election year into the four crucial periods which comprise it.

Nominating convention in July or August to election day in November. No law states what would happen if either a President-nominate or a Vice-President-nominate were to die or withdraw before election day, but both the Republican and Democratic parties have adopted clear-cut procedures to cover such eventualities. (Note that this is not a hypothetical problem. In 1860 the Democratic party legally nominated Senator Benjamin Fitzpatrick of Alabama to be Vice-President, but after the convention had adjourned and its members dispersed, Fitzpatrick refused to accept the nomination and the party was left without a candidate.)

The rules of the two parties are different. The Republican party authorizes its national committee to fill the vacancy, with each state or territory's delegates empowered to cast the same number of votes it had at that year's nominating convention. Alternatively, the national committee may choose to summon a new convention, should such a step seem preferable, and if the vacancy has occurred early enough in this period to permit the reconvening of the convention. The mood and temper of the political situation within the party and nation would also be taken into account in choosing between these two alternatives.

The Democratic party provides only the first option, that the national committee shall have the power to fill the vacancy, with each state or territory having its allotted votes.

Both national committees retain the right to fill a vacancy in the Presidential spot by the simple device of moving up the Vice-President-nominate and designating a new candidate for the Vice-Presidency. For example, had the Democrats won in 1968 and had Humphrey died, they could have elevated Edmund S. Muskie to the Presidential spot and then chosen a new Vice-President, and I suppose the Democratic electors would have accepted this.

This group of arrangements seems simple, workable, and just. Should death or vacancy occur a few days before the election, there would of course be chaos, but I do not see how this could be avoided in any system; that party on whom the blow fell would have to adjust to it as best it could. Incidentally, in 1860, when Senator Fitzpatrick threw the Democratic nomination back into the teeth of the party, the leaders calmly selected someone else in accordance with the procedures outlined above for that party.

And in 1912 Vice-President James S. Sherman, after he had been legally nominated by the Republican party and was running for re-election, died a few days before election. The Republican National Committee, meeting in crash session, designated Nicholas Murray Butler as his replacement, a substitution which was amicably accepted both by the voters and the Republican electors, who had earlier been pledged to Sherman.

I would assume from these precedents, and from the clarity of the bylaws governing the two major parties, that accidents within this period can be handled expeditiously and in a manner which the public will accept. There is no federal law, however, sanctioning these procedures and perhaps there ought to be, except that most of the operations of our political parties are not the subject of public law.

Election day in November to the vote of the Electoral College in December. It seems clear beyond contention that should a President-designate die or withdraw in this period, the electors would be free to vote for whomever they wished. Eligible citizens of the entire nation, irrespective of party, would be possible candidates, but obviously every effort would be made to keep the electors committed to voting for whomever the party officials nominated. Those nominations would be made in accordance with the rules cited earlier, in view of the fact that legally the election had not been completed in November and would not be until the Electoral College had met. If the substitute designated by the party were reasonably acceptable to the electors, it would be logical for them to support the party, for to do otherwise would bring down upon them a heavy burden of opprobrium. But it must be repeated that under our system these faceless electors, chosen arbitrarily and at random, would have the obligation to elect a President and the freedom to choose whom they wished. This is an extraordinary delegation of powers that not one American in a hundred thousand realizes he has made.

Vote of the Electoral College in December to vote-counting and certifying in Congress on January 6. Should a President-elect die or withdraw during this period, there would be debate as to what should happen. Some have argued that the Greeley precedent would apply and that Congress would again refuse to count votes belonging to a dead man, but the analogy is not good. Greeley died before the Electoral College met, so that the electors were voting for a man they knew to be dead; in the case represented by this paragraph, the electors would have voted for a living man, who had subsequently died, but who was entitled at the time of voting to all votes cast on his behalf. Most constitutional experts believe that the language of the Twelfth Amendment supersedes this tradition and gives Congress no choice but to count all electoral votes cast, provided the man voted for was alive when the electoral ballots were cast. The House of Representatives committee report endorsing the Twentieth Amendment sustains this view but has not the force of law. Congress, this report said, could exercise no discretion in the matter and would declare that the dead candidate had received a majority of the votes. The operative law would then be the Twentieth Amendment, Section 3, which states: "If, at the time fixed for the beginning of the term of the President, the President-elect shall have died, the Vice-President-elect shall become President." Mark Gruell, Pennsylvania's parliamentarian, has made a study of these problems, and states, "Under present law, the electoral votes must still be counted and declared in Congress. It would therefore be the President-elect who had died, and the Vice-President-elect would become President." Furthermore, when the Vice-President-elect did take office as President, he would be authorized under the Twenty-fifth Amendment to nominate a new Vice-President. The ambiguities that arise in this time period could easily be clarified.

Vote-counting and certifying in Congress on January 6 to inauguration on January 20. Here the laws are clear without question. Should the President-elect die in this interval, the foregoing provisions of the Twentieth Amendment would elevate the Vice-President-elect to the Presidency. Should the Vice-President-elect die in this interval, the Twenty-fifth Amendment authorizes the new President, upon taking office, to nominate a new Vice-President, subject to confirmation by the House and Senate. The admirable clarity of this law should be extended to the entire process, and this could easily be done.

Whatever conclusion one reaches in trying to fathom the constellation of incongruities in this lottery, he must in the end decide that this is the silliest instrument of self-government that sensible men could devise; and it stands out with special prominence because the rest of our system is so rational.

I think it peculiar that free men would hesitate to change something palpably wrong out of respect for the Founding Fathers of this nation, when those Fathers, finding themselves faced by a part of their invention that did not work, had no hesitancy in initiating steps to junk it, and this within twelve years of when they launched the system. The first election held under the plan adopted by Washington, Madison, Hamilton, and Franklin took place in 1789, and since Washington was elected unanimously, there was no problem. The 1792 election was equally smooth, and in 1796, when everyone understood that John Adams was intended to succeed, the system once more functioned, but in 1800, as we have seen, the Jefferson-Burr election resulted in chaos, and within the quickest possible time the very men who had framed the election system altered it, offered the nation an amendment, and rammed the change through in time for the 1804 election.

If the Founding Fathers were alive today, if they could see the idiotic mess into which their invention of electors and House elections has led us, they would abolish both before the 1972 election was held. They would whip up an amendment and campaign for it across the nation, because to do otherwise would be illogical, and they were not illogical men.

It was with these thoughts that I watched this tangled election come to its fumbling conclusion. As the year ended I gave thanks that what could have ended so poorly had ended so well. But on Friday, January 3, 1969, a dramatic event erupted, proving to me that the election was not going to end as peacefully as I had thought, and proving to the American people just how great the peril was through which they had been passing.

On this day Senator Edmund S. Muskie, Democrat of Maine, and Representative James G. O'Hara, Democrat of Michigan, announced that they intended to institute a procedure which would dramatize for the American people the perils inherent in the Electoral College.

Their strategy was this. When the reports from the states were opened in the joint session of Congress on January 6, they intended to invoke a never-before-used clause from the election law of 1887, which had come into being to correct the abuses uncovered in the Hayes-Tilden deadlock of 1876. Under this law, they would challenge the renegade electoral vote cast by Dr. Lloyd W. Bailey of North Carolina, who had run on the Republican ticket, been elected on that ticket, but who had decided on his own initiative to ignore the mandate of the voters and to cast his vote not for Nixon, who had carried North Carolina (627,192 Nixon; 496,188 Wallace; 464,113 Humphrey), but for Wallace.

Thus two Democrats would try to force an elector to vote for a Republican instead of for a third-party candidate, and in so doing would focus the attention of the nation upon a glaring weakness in our electoral system. In this respect their action was a laudable illustration of high-minded and unselfish statesmanship.

But apparently they were unaware that the 1887 law gave Congress no authority to challenge the propriety of an electoral vote once it had been cast, duly recorded and accurately reported to Congress. Therefore, what Muskie proposed was that Congress adopt illegal procedures to correct an evil which existed only because Congress had refused for so many decades to tackle election reform.

It was also amusing to hear him castigate Dr. Bailey as "the faithless elector." Faithless to what? To the Constitution? No, because this document allows the kind of procedure which Dr. Bailey had followed. Faithless to the laws of North Carolina? No, because the majority of our states (including North Carolina) have refused to try to bind their electors, the suspicions being great that such efforts would be illegal and fruitless. Faithless to tradition? No, because in recent years it had become common for electors to vote contrary to the way their states had voted, and in this freedom they had been confirmed both by popular opinion and by lack of prosecution. I judge that what Senator Muskie must have meant was faithless to what Congress vaguely intended but was too indifferent to enact into law, and to such shadowy precepts one should be faithless.

On January 6, 1969, Congress met in joint session to receive from the fifty states and the District of Columbia their reports as to how their electors had voted. As planned, Muskie and O'Hara challenged the North Carolina vote, and as spelled out in the 1887 law, the two houses promptly separated to weigh the challenge. The discussion was enlightening.

The debate had not progressed far in the Senate before it became clear that over the weekend the sponsors of the challenge had done some homework regarding the law of 1887. They had found that whereas it provided a rather nebulous base for challenging a state's report of its votes, it provided none whatever for challenging the right of an elector to vote as he preferred. Most specifically, once an elector had so voted, his vote could not be transferred to another candidate. Consequently, the high moral purpose of the challenge was abandoned; it was no longer two public-spirited Democrats fighting to give Richard Nixon another vote, for that was impossible. It now became a procedure for disciplining a refractory elector, and that too proved impossible.

Many speakers pointed out that whereas they were going to have to vote against the challenge, which meant that they were supporting the right of any elector to vote as he pleased, they were morally opposed to such behavior and would support legislation or amendment which would end the practice. Thus Muskie and O'Hara achieved much of their intention if little of their motion; legislators were publicly committing themselves to reform.

The salient victory, however, came in an unexpected quarter. Senator Everett McKinley Dirksen of Illinois, leader of the Senate Republicans, declared that in his opinion "electoral reform legislation is virtually inevitable" in Congress this year. On the motion before the Senate, however, he voted against the Muskie challenge, pointing out that he did not intend to approach changes in the system of electing Presidents on a piecemeal basis. In each of these attitudes he seemed to reflect the opinions of many, in both the Senate and the House.

When the time came to vote, the two houses did what the law required: they accepted the North Carolina vote for Wallace as cast, the Senate 58–33, the House 229–169. However, as Muskie ruefully pointed out to a press conference after adjournment, "The elector has now been liberated to an extent that he has not been free to act in one hundred years." This charge was misleading.

It has been the argument of this essay that the elector has enjoyed this freedom since 1789 and that at any point in that long and hazardous period the Supreme Court would have had to uphold the elector in his exercise of that freedom. But Muskie is correct in pointing out that Congressional action on January 6, 1969, did confirm the right and did establish a precedent which might mean that later instances of elector revolt need not be taken to the Supreme Court. Congress has settled the matter inadvertently, but in doing so, has merely confirmed what serious critics have suspected all along.

It now seems clear that if the November vote had produced a deadlock in the Electoral College, whatever maneuvers Governor Wallace might have engaged in to dictate a winner would have been upheld by Congress, and probably by the Supreme Court had the case gone so far. It also seems clear that whatever maneuvers we Republican and Democratic electors might have devised among ourselves to forestall Wallace would also have been upheld.

The crucial significance of the Muskie challenge lay not in this clarification of Congressional and perhaps court attitude toward self-willed electors, but in its tacit invitation to mass revolt in the future. In the past, many electors must have felt inclined to vote as they pleased, but refrained through fear of unknown consequences; now they could be sure that there would be no consequences. I judge that when Congress voted to sustain the arbitrary North Carolina elector, our nation moved into a position two or three times more perilous than the one it had occupied the day before.

Therefore, in this essay I have not been speculating about abstract possibilities; I have been dealing with a deadly serious reality: the political security of our nation. If one seeks a compelling reason for immediate reform, the Congressional confirmation of the North Carolina vote provides it.

During a period of more than a year—from mid-August of 1967, when I debated in my constituency as a candidate to the Constitutional Convention, through mid-December of 1968, when I served as an elector—I had thought principally about the problems that face a free society when it seeks to govern itself. In the last four months I had thought only of the Electoral College and the potential election in the House of Representatives, and in all that time of careful study I never read or heard or thought of a single argument in favor of retaining these two anachronisms.

They must be abolished. They must be abolished now. They must be abolished before they wreck our democracy.

APPENDICES

APPENDIX A

THE CONSTITUTION
OF THE
UNITED STATES
OF AMERICA

ARTICLE II

SECTION 1. The executive Power shall be vested in a President of the United States of America. He shall hold his Office during the Term of four years, and, together with the Vice-President, chosen for the same Term, be elected, as follows:

Each State shall appoint, in such Manner as the Legislature thereof may direct, a Number of Electors, equal to the whole Number of Senators and Representatives to which the State may be entitled in the Congress: but no Senator or Representative, or Person holding an Office of Trust or Profit under the United States, shall be appointed an Elector.

[The Electors shall meet in their respective States, and vote by Ballot for two persons, of whom one at least shall not be an Inhabitant of the same State with themselves. And they shall make a List of all the Persons voted for, and of the Number of Votes for each; which List they shall sign and certify, and transmit sealed to the Seat of the Government of the United States, directed to the President of the Senate. The President of the Senate shall, in the Presence of the Senate and House of Representatives, open all the Certificates, and the Votes shall then be counted. The Person having the greatest Number of Votes shall be the President, if such Number be a Majority of the whole Number of Electors appointed; and if there be more than one who have such Majority, and have an equal Number of Votes, then the House of Representatives shall immediately chuse by Ballot one of them for President; and if no Person have a Majority, then from the five highest on the List the said House shall in like Manner chuse the President. But in chusing the President, the Votes shall be taken by States, the Representation from each State having one Vote; a quorum for this Purpose shall consist of a Member or Members from two-thirds of the States, and a Majority of all the States shall be necessary to a Choice. In every Case, after the Choice of the President, the Person having the greatest Number of Votes of the Electors shall be the Vice President. But if there should remain two or more who have equal votes, the Senate shall chuse from them by Ballot the Vice-President.]*

The Congress may determine the Time of chusing the Electors, and the Day on which they shall give their Votes; which Day shall be the same throughout the United States.

No person except a natural-born Citizen, or a Citizen of the United States, at the time of the Adoption of this Constitution, shall be eligible to the Office of President; neither shall any Person be eligible to that Office who shall not have attained to the Age of thirty-five years, and been fourteen Years a Resident within the United States.

In Case of the Removal of the President from Office, or of his Death, Resignation, or Inability to discharge the Powers and Duties of the said Office, the same shall devolve on the Vice President, and the Congress may by Law provide for the Case of Removal, Death, Resignation, or Inability, both of the President and Vice President, declaring what Officer shall then act as President, and such Officer shall act accordingly, until the disability be removed, or a President shall be elected.

The President shall, at stated Times, receive for his Services a Compensation, which shall neither be increased nor diminished during the Period for which he shall have been elected, and he shall not receive within that Period any other Emolument from the United States, or any of them.

Before he enter on the execution of his Office, he shall take the following Oath or Affirmation:—"I do solemnly swear (or affirm)

*Revised by 12th Amendment.

that I will faithfully execute the Office of President of the United States, and will, to the best of my ability, preserve, protect, and defend the Constitution of the United States."

SECTION 2. The President shall be Commander in Chief of the Army and Navy of the United States, and of the Militia of the several States, when called into the actual Service of the United States; he may require the Opinion, in writing, of the principal Officer in each of the executive Departments, upon any subject relating to the Duties of their respective Offices, and he shall have Power to Grant Reprieves and Pardons for Offenses against the United States, except in Cases of Impeachment.

He shall have Power, by and with the Advice and Consent of the Senate, to make Treaties, provided two thirds of the Senators present concur; and he shall nominate, and by and with the Advice and Consent of the Senate, shall appoint Ambassadors, other public Ministers and Consuls, Judges of the Supreme Court, and all other Officers of the United States, whose Appointments are not herein otherwise provided for, and which shall be established by Law: but the Congress may by Law vest the Appointment of such inferior Officers, as they think proper, in the President alone, in the Courts of Law, or in the Heads of Departments.

The President shall have Power to fill up all Vacancies that may happen during the Recess of the Senate, by granting Commissions which shall expire at the End of their next Session.

SECTION 3. He shall from time to time give to the Congress Information of the State of the Union, and recommend to their Consideration such Measures as he shall judge necessary and expedient; he may, on extraordinary occasions, convene both Houses, or either of them, and in Case of Disagreement between them, with respect to the Time of Adjournment, he may adjourn them to such Time as he shall think proper; he shall receive Ambassadors and other public Ministers; he shall take Care that the Laws be faithfully executed, and shall Commission all the Officers of the United States.

SECTION 4. The President, Vice President and all civil Officers of the United States, shall be removed from Office on Impeachment for, and Conviction of, Treason, Bribery, or other high Crimes and Misdemeanors.

AMENDMENT 12
(Ratified July 27, 1804)

The Electors shall meet in their respective States and vote by ballot for President and Vice-President, one of whom, at least, shall not be an inhabitant of the same State with themselves; they shall name in their ballots the person voted for as President, and in distinct ballots the person voted for as Vice-President, and they shall make distinct lists of all persons voted for as President, and of all persons voted for as Vice-President, and of the number of votes for each, which lists they shall sign and certify, and transmit sealed to the seat of the government of the United States, directed to the President of the Senate;—The President of the Senate shall, in the presence of the Senate and House of Representatives, open all the certificates and the votes shall then be counted;—The person having the greatest number of votes for President, shall be the President, if such number be a majority of the whole number of Electors appointed; and if no person have such majority, then from the persons having the highest numbers not exceeding three on the list of those voted for as President, the House of Representatives shall choose immediately, by ballot, the President. But in choosing the President, the votes shall be taken by states, the representation from each state having one vote; a quorum for this purpose shall consist of a member or members from two-thirds of the states, and a majority of all the states shall be necessary to a choice. And if the House of Representatives shall not choose a President whenever the right of choice shall devolve upon them, before the fourth day of March next following, then the Vice-President shall act as President, as in the case of the death or other constitutional disability of the President.—The person having the greatest number of votes as Vice-President, shall be the Vice-President, if such number be a majority of the whole number of Electors appointed, and if no person have a majority, then from the two highest numbers on the list, the Senate shall choose the Vice-President; a quorum for the purpose shall consist of two-thirds of the whole number of Senators, and a majority of the whole number shall be necessary to a choice. But no person constitutionally ineligible to the office of President shall be eligible to that of Vice-President of the United States.

AMENDMENT 20
(Ratified January 23, 1933)

SECTION 1. The terms of the President and Vice-President shall end at noon on the 20th day of January, and the terms of Senators and Representatives at noon on the 3d day of January, of the years in which such terms would have ended if this article had not been ratified; and the terms of their successors shall then begin.

SECTION 2. The Congress shall assemble at least once in every year, and such meeting shall begin at noon on the 3d day of January, unless they shall by law appoint a different day.

SECTION 3. If, at the time fixed for the beginning of the term of the President, the President elect shall have died, the Vice-President elect shall become President. If a President shall not have been chosen before the time fixed for the beginning of his term, or if the President elect shall have failed to qualify, then the Vice-President elect shall act as President until a President shall have qualified; and the Congress may by law provide for the case wherein neither a President elect nor a Vice-President elect shall have qualified, declaring who shall then act as President, or the manner in which one who is to act shall be selected, and such person shall act accordingly until a President or Vice-President shall have qualified.

SECTION 4. The Congress may by law provide for the case of the death of any of the persons from whom the House of Representatives may choose a President whenever the right of choice shall have devolved upon them, and for the case of the death of any of the persons from whom the Senate may choose a Vice-President whenever the right of choice shall have devolved upon them.

SECTION 5. Sections 1 and 2 shall take effect on the 15th day of October following the ratification of this article.

SECTION 6. This article shall be inoperative unless it shall have been ratified as an amendment to the Constitution by the legislatures of three-fourths of the several States within seven years from the date of its submission.

AMENDMENT 22
(Ratified February 27, 1951)

SECTION 1. No person shall be elected to the office of the President more than twice, and no person who has held the office of President, or acted as President, for more than two years of a term to which some other person was elected President shall be elected to the office of the President more than once.

But this Article shall not apply to any person holding the office of President when this article was proposed by the Congress, and shall not prevent any person who may be holding the office of President, or acting as President, during the term within which this Article becomes operative from holding the office of President or acting as President during the remainder of such term.

SECTION 2. This article shall be inoperative unless it shall have been ratified as an amendment to the Constitution by the legislatures of three-fourths of the several states within seven years from the date of its submission to the states by the Congress.

AMENDMENT 23
(Ratified March 29, 1961)

SECTION 1. The District constituting the seat of Government of the United States shall appoint in such manner as the Congress may direct:

A number of electors of President and Vice-President equal to the whole number of Senators and Representatives in Congress to which the District would be entitled if it were a State, but in no event more than the least populous State; they shall be in addition to those appointed by the States, but they shall be considered, for the purposes of the election of President and Vice-President, to be electors appointed by a State; and they shall meet in the District and perform such duties as provided by the twelfth article of amendment.

SECTION 2. The Congress shall have power to enforce this article by appropriate legislation.

AMENDMENT 25
(Ratified February 10, 1967)

SECTION 1. In case of the removal of the President from office or of his death or resignation, the Vice President shall become President.

SECTION 2. Whenever there is a vacancy in the office of the Vice President, the President shall nominate a Vice President who shall take office upon confirmation by a majority vote of both Houses of Congress.

SECTION 3. Whenever the President transmits to the President Pro Tempore of the Senate and the Speaker of the House of Representatives his written declaration that he is unable to discharge the powers and duties of his office, and until he transmits to them a written declaration to the contrary, such powers and duties shall be discharged by the Vice President as Acting President.

SECTION 4. Whenever the Vice President and a majority of either the principal officers of the executive departments or of such other body as Congress may by law provide, transmit to the President Pro Tempore of the Senate and the Speaker of the House of Representatives their written declaration that the President is unable to discharge the powers and duties of his office, the Vice President shall immediately assume the powers and duties of the office as Acting President.

Thereafter, when the President transmits to the President Pro Tempore of the Senate and the Speaker of the House of Representatives his written declaration that no inability exists, he shall resume the powers and duties of his office unless the Vice President and a majority of either the principal officers of the executive department or of such other body as Congress may by law provide, transmit within four days to the President Pro Tempore of the Senate and the Speaker of the House of Representatives their written declaration that the President is unable to discharge the powers and duties of his office. Thereupon Congress shall decide the issue, assembling within forty-eight hours for that purpose if not in session. If the Congress, within twenty-one days after receipt of the latter written declaration, or, if Congress is not in session, within twenty-one days after Congress is required to assemble, determines by two-thirds vote of both Houses that the President is unable to discharge the powers and duties of his office, the Vice President shall continue to discharge the same as Acting President; otherwise, the President shall resume the powers and duties of his office.

APPENDIX B

PROPOSED AMENDMENTS TO THE CONSTITUTION

1. THE AUTOMATIC PLAN

[Text of proposed amendment to the Constitution, introduced Jan. 3, 1969, by Rep. Hale Boggs (D., La.) and others.]

Section 1. The executive power shall be vested in a President of the United States of America. He shall hold his office during the term of four years, and together with the Vice President chosen for the same term, be elected as provided in this Constitution.

The President and Vice President shall be elected by the people of each State in such manner as the legislature thereof may direct, and by the people of the District constituting the seat of the Government of the United States (hereafter in this article referred to as the "District") in such manner as the Congress shall by law prescribe. The Congress may determine the time of the election of the President and Vice President, which day shall be the same throughout the United States. In such an election, a vote may be cast only as a joint vote for the election of two persons (referred to in this article as a "presidential candidacy") one of whom has consented that his name appear as candidate for President on the ballot with the name of the other as candidate for Vice President, and the other of whom has consented that his name appear as candidate for Vice President on the ballot with the name of the said candidate for President. No person may consent to have his name appear on the ballot with more than one other person. No person constitutionally ineligible to the office of President shall be eligible to that of Vice President. In each State and in the District the official custodian of election returns shall make distinct lists of all presidential candidacies for which votes were cast, and of the number of votes in such State for each candidacy, which lists he shall sign and certify and transmit to the seat of the Government of the United States, directed to the President of the Senate. The President of the Senate shall, in the presence of the Senate and House of Representatives, open all the certificates and the electoral votes shall be computed in the manner provided in section 2.

Section 2. Each State shall be entitled to a number of electoral votes for each of the offices of President and Vice President equal to the whole number of Senators and Representatives to which such State may be entitled in the Congress. The District shall be entitled to a number of electoral votes for each such office equal to the whole number of Senators and Representatives in Congress to which the District would be entitled if it were a State, but in no event more than the least populous State. In the case of each State and the District, the presidential candidacy receiving the greatest number of votes shall be entitled to the whole number of the electoral votes of such State or District. If a presidential candidacy receives a plurality of at least 40 per centum of the electoral votes, the persons comprising such candidacy shall be the President-elect and the Vice President-elect. If no presidential candidacy receives a plurality of at least 40 per centum of the electoral votes, a run-off election shall be conducted, in such manner as the Congress shall by law prescribe, between the two presidential candidacies which receive the greatest number of electoral votes. The persons comprising the candidacy which receives the greatest number of electoral votes in such election shall become the President-elect and the Vice President-elect.

Section 3. The Congress shall by law provide procedures to be followed in consequence of the death or withdrawal of a candidate on or before the date of an election under this article, or in the case of a tie.

Section 4. The twelfth article of amendment to the Constitution, the twenty-third article of amendment to the Constitution, the first four paragraphs of section 1, article II of the Constitution, and section 4 of the twentieth article of amendment to the Constitution are repealed.

Section 5. This article shall not apply to any election of the President or Vice President for a term of office beginning earlier than one year after the date of ratification of this article.

2. THE DISTRICT PLAN

[Text of proposed amendment to the Constitution, introduced Jan. 15, 1969, by Sen. Karl Mundt (R., S.D.) and others.]

Section 1. Each State shall choose a number of Electors of President and Vice President equal to the whole number of Senators and Representatives to which the State may be entitled in the Congress; but no Senator or Representative, or person holding an office of trust or profit under the United States, shall be chosen an Elector.

The Electors assigned to each State with its Senators shall be elected by the people thereof. Each of the Electors apportioned with its Representatives shall be elected by the people of a single-member electoral district formed by the legislature of the State. Electoral districts within each State shall be of compact and contiguous territory containing substantially equal numbers of inhabitants, and shall not be altered until another census of the United States has been taken. Each candidate for the office of Elector of President and Vice President shall file in writing under oath a declaration of the identity of the persons for whom he will vote for President and Vice President, which declaration shall be binding upon any successor to his office. In choosing Electors the voters in each State shall have the qualifications requisite for Electors of the most numerous branch of the State legislature.

The Electors shall meet in their respective States, fill any vacancies in their number as directed by the State legislature, and vote by signed ballot for President and Vice President, one of whom, at least, shall not be an inhabitant of the same State with themselves; they shall name in their ballots the person voted for as President, and in distinct ballots the person voted for as Vice President; and they shall make distinct lists of all persons voted for as President, and of all persons voted for as Vice President, the number of votes for each, and the name and electoral district, if any, of each Elector who cast his vote for each such person, which lists they shall sign and certify, and transmit sealed to the seat of government of the United States, directed to the President of the Senate. The President of the Senate shall, in the presence of the Senate and the House of Representatives, open all the certificates and the votes shall then be counted. Any vote cast by an elector contrary to the declaration made by him shall be counted as a vote cast in accordance with his declaration. The person having the greatest number of electoral votes for President shall be the President, and the person having the greatest number of electoral votes for Vice President shall be the Vice President, if such numbers are a majority of the whole number of Electors chosen. If two persons have the same total number of electoral votes, which number is one-half of the whole number of Electors chosen, the person having the greatest number of votes cast by Electors chosen from electoral districts shall be President, or Vice President, as the case may be.

If no person voted for as President has such a majority, then from the persons having the three highest numbers of votes for President, the Senate and House of Representatives together, each member having one vote, shall choose immediately, by ballot, the President. A quorum for such purpose shall be three-fourths of the whole number of the Senators and Representatives, and a majority of the whole number shall be necessary to a choice. If an additional ballot is necessary, the choice on the second ballot shall be between the two persons having the highest numbers of votes on the first ballot.

If no person voted for as Vice President has such a majority, then the Vice President shall be chosen from the persons having the three highest numbers of votes for Vice President in the same manner as herein provided for choosing the President. But no person constitutionally ineligible to the office of President shall be eligible to that of Vice President of the United States.

Section 2. The Congress shall have power to carry this article into effect by appropriate legislation. The Congress may provide by law for the determination of questions concerning breach of faith by Electors in the casting of electoral votes, and for the case of the death of any of the persons from whom the Senate and the House of Representatives may choose a President or a Vice President whenever the right of choice shall have devolved upon them.

Section 3. This article supersedes the second and third paragraphs of Section 1, Article II, of the Constitution, the Twelfth Article of

Amendment to the Constitution, and Section 4 of the Twentieth Article of Amendment to the Constitution.

Section 4. Electors appointed pursuant to the Twenty-third Article of Amendment to this Constitution shall be elected by the people of such district in such manner as the Congress may direct. Candidates for Elector and Electors of such district shall have the same obligations, and shall perform the same duties, as candidates for Elector and Electors of the several States under this article.

Section 5. This article shall take effect on the 4th day of July following its ratification.

3. THE PROPORTIONAL PLAN

[Text of proposed amendment to the Constitution, introduced Jan. 15, 1969, by Sen. Sam J. Ervin, Jr. (D., N.C.) and others.]

Section 1. The Executive power shall be vested in a President of the United States of America. He shall hold his office during the term of four years, and, together with the Vice President, chosen for the same term, be elected as provided in this Constitution.

The office of elector of the President and Vice President, as established by section 1 of article II of this Constitution and the twelfth and twenty-third articles of amendment to this Constitution, is hereby abolished. The President and Vice President shall be elected by the people of the several States and the District constituting the seat of government of the United States. The electors in each State shall have the qualifications requisite for electors of the most numerous branch of the State legislature, except that the legislature of any State may prescribe lesser qualifications with respect to residence therein. The electors in such District shall have such qualifications as the Congress may prescribe. The places and manner of holding such election in each State shall be prescribed by the legislature thereof; but the Congress may at any time by law make or alter such regulations. The place and manner of holding such election in such District shall be prescribed by the Congress. Congress shall determine the time of such election, which shall be the same throughout the United States. Until otherwise determined by the Congress, such election shall be held on the Tuesday next after the first Monday in November of the year preceding the year in which the regular term of the President is to begin. Each State shall be entitled to a number of electoral votes equal to the whole number of Senators and Representatives to which such State may be entitled in the Congress. Such District shall be entitled to a number of electoral votes equal to the whole number of Senators and Representatives in Congress to which such District would be entitled if it were a State, but in no event more than the least populous State.

Within forty-five days after such election, or at such time as Congress shall direct, the official custodian of the election returns of each State and such District shall make distinct lists of all persons for whom votes were cast for President and the number of votes for each, and the total vote of the electors of the State or the District for all persons for President, which lists he shall sign and certify and transmit sealed to the seat of the Government of the United States, directed to the President of the Senate. On the sixth day of January following the election, unless the Congress by law appoints a different day not earlier than the fourth day of January and not later than the tenth day of January, the President of the Senate shall, in the presence of the Senate and House of Representatives, open all certificates and the votes shall then be counted. Each person for whom votes were cast for President in each State and such District shall be credited with such proportion of the electoral votes thereof as he received of the total vote of the electors therein for President. In making the computation, fractional numbers less than one one-thousandth shall be disregarded. The person having the greatest number of electoral votes for President shall be President, if such number be at least 40 per centum of the whole number of such electoral votes. If no person has received at least 40 per centum of the whole number of electoral votes, or if two persons have received an identical number of electoral votes which is at least 40 per centum of the whole number of electoral votes, then from the persons having the two greatest numbers of electoral votes for President, the Senate and the House of Representatives sitting in joint session shall choose immediately, by ballot, the President. A majority of the votes of the combined authorized membership of the Senate and the House of Representatives shall be necessary for a choice.

The Vice President shall be likewise elected, at the same time and in the same manner and subject to the same provisions, as the President, but no person constitutionally ineligible for the office of

President shall be eligible to that of Vice President of the United States.

The Congress may by law provide for the case of the death of any of the persons from whom the Senate and the House of Representatives may choose a President whenever the right of choice shall have devolved upon them, and for the case of death of any of the persons from whom the Senate and the House of Representatives may choose a Vice President whenever the right of choice shall have devolved upon them. The Congress shall have power to enforce this article by appropriate legislation.

Section 2. This article shall take effect on the tenth day of February next after one year shall have elapsed following its ratification.

4. DIRECT POPULAR VOTE

[Text of proposed amendment to the Constitution, introduced Jan. 15, 1969, by Sen. Birch Bayh (D., Ind.) and others.]

Section 1. The people of the several States and the District constituting the seat of Government of the United States shall be the electors of the President and Vice President. In such elections, each elector shall cast a single vote for two persons who shall have consented to the joining of their names on the ballot for the offices of President and Vice President. No persons shall consent to their name being joined with that of more than one other person.

Section 2. The electors in each State shall have the qualifications requisite for the electors of members of the Congress from that State, except that any State may adopt less restrictive residence requirements for voting for President and Vice President than for members of Congress and Congress may adopt uniform residence and age requirements for voting in such elections. The Congress shall prescribe the qualifications for electors from the District of Columbia.

Section 3. The persons joined as candidates for President and Vice President, having the greatest number of votes shall be declared elected President and Vice President, if such number be at least 40 per centum of the total number of votes certified. If none of the persons joined as candidates for President and Vice President shall have at least 40 per centum of the total number of votes certified, a runoff election shall be held between the two pairs of persons joined as candidates for President and Vice President who received the highest number of votes certified.

Section 4. The days for such elections shall be determined by Congress and shall be the same throughout the United States. The times, places, and manner of holding such elections and entitlement to inclusion on the ballot shall be prescribed in each State by the legislature thereof; but the Congress may at any time by law make or alter such regulations. The times, places, and manner of holding such elections and entitlement to inclusion on the ballot shall be prescribed by the Congress for such elections in the District of Columbia.

Section 5. The Congress shall prescribe by law the time, place, and manner in which the results of such elections shall be ascertained and declared.

Section 6. If, at the time fixed for the counting of the certified vote totals from the respective States, the presidential candidate who would have been entitled to election as President shall have died, the vice presidential candidate entitled to election as Vice President shall be declared elected President.

The Congress may by law provide for the case of the death or withdrawal of any candidate or candidates for President and Vice President and for the case of the death of both the President-elect and Vice President-elect and, further, the Congress may by law provide for the case of a tie.

Section 7. The Congress shall have power to enforce this article by appropriate legislation.

Section 8. This article shall take effect on the 1st day of May following its ratification.

APPENDIX C

THE BANZHAF STUDIES

1. THE AUTOMATIC PLAN

State Name (1)	Population 1960 Census	Electoral Vote 1968	Relative Voting Power (2)	Percent Excess Voting Power (3)	Percent Deviation From Average Voting Power (4)
Ala.	3266740.	10	1.632	63.2	—3.0
Alaska	226167.	3	1.838	83.8	9.2
Ariz.	1302161.	5	1.281	28.1	—23.9
Ark.	1786272.	6	1.315	31.5	—21.9
Calif.	15717204.	40	3.162	216.2	87.9
Colo.	1753947.	6	1.327	32.7	—21.1
Conn.	2535234.	8	1.477	47.7	—12.2
Del.	446292.	3	1.308	30.8	—22.3
D. C.	763956.	3	1.000	.0	—40.6
Fla.	4951560.	14	1.870	87.0	11.1
Ga.	3943116.	12	1.789	78.9	6.3
Hawaii	632772.	4	1.468	46.8	—12.8
Idaho	667191.	4	1.429	42.9	—15.1
Ill.	10081158.	26	2.491	149.1	48.0
Ind.	4662498.	13	1.786	78.6	6.1
Iowa	2757537.	9	1.596	59.6	—5.2
Kansas	2178611.	7	1.392	39.2	—17.3
Ky.	3038156.	9	1.521	52.1	—9.6
La.	3257022.	10	1.635	63.5	—2.9
Maine	969265.	4	1.186	18.6	—29.5
Md.	3100689.	10	1.675	67.5	—.4
Mass.	5148578.	14	1.834	83.4	9.0
Mich.	7823194.	21	2.262	126.2	34.4
Minn.	3413864.	10	1.597	59.7	—5.1
Miss.	2178141.	7	1.392	39.2	—17.3

State Name (1)	Population 1960 Census	Electoral Vote 1968	Relative Voting Power (2)	Percent Excess Voting Power (3)	Percent Deviation From Average Voting Power (4)
Mo.	4319813.	12	1.710	71.0	1.6
Mont.	674767.	4	1.421	42.1	—15.5
Neb.	1411330.	5	1.231	23.1	—26.9
Nev.	285278.	3	1.636	63.6	—2.8
N. H.	606921.	4	1.499	49.9	—10.9
N. J.	6066782.	17	2.063	106.3	22.6
N. M.	951023.	4	1.197	19.7	—28.9
N. Y.	16782304.	43	3.312	231.2	96.8
N. C.	4556155.	13	1.807	80.7	7.4
N. D.	632446.	4	1.468	46.8	—12.8
Ohio	9706397.	26	2.539	153.9	50.9
Okla.	2328284.	8	1.541	54.1	—8.4
Ore.	1768687.	6	1.321	32.1	—21.5
Pa.	11319366.	29	2.638	163.8	56.8
R. I.	859488.	4	1.259	25.9	—25.2
S. C.	2382594.	8	1.524	52.4	—9.5
S. D.	680514.	4	1.415	41.5	—15.9
Tenn.	3567089.	11	1.721	72.1	2.3
Texas	9579677.	25	2.452	145.2	45.7
Utah	890627.	4	1.237	23.7	—26.5
Vt.	389881.	3	1.400	40.0	—16.8
Va.	3966949.	12	1.784	78.4	6.0
Wash.	2853214.	9	1.569	56.9	—6.8
W. Va.	1860421.	7	1.506	50.6	—10.5
Wis.	3951777.	12	1.788	78.8	6.2
Wyo.	330066.	3	1.521	52.1	—9.6

(1) Includes the District of Columbia.

(2) Ratio of voting power of citizens of state compared with voters of the most deprived state.

(3) Percent by which voting power exceeds that of the most deprived voters (deviations).

(4) Percent by which voting power deviated from the average of the figures in column 4.

Minus signs indicate less than average voting power.

2. THE PROPORTIONAL PLAN

State Name (1)	Population 1960 Census	Electoral Vote 1968	Relative Voting Power (2)	Percent Excess Voting Power (3)	Percent Deviation From Average Voting Power (4)
Ala.	3266740.	10	1.203	20.3	−26.5
Alaska	226167.	3	5.212	421.2	218.7
Ariz.	1302161.	5	1.509	50.9	−7.7
Ark.	1786272.	6	1.320	32.0	−19.3
Calif.	15717204.	40	1.000	.0	−38.9
Colo.	1753947.	6	1.344	34.4	−17.8
Conn.	2535234.	8	1.240	24.0	−24.2
Del.	446292.	3	2.641	164.1	61.5
D. C.	763956.	3	1.543	54.3	−5.6
Fla.	4951560.	14	1.111	11.1	−32.1
Ga.	3943116.	12	1.196	19.6	−26.9
Hawaii	632772.	4	2.484	148.4	51.9
Idaho	667191.	4	2.356	135.6	44.0
Ill.	10081158.	26	1.013	1.3	−38.0
Ind.	4662498.	13	1.096	9.6	−33.0
Iowa	2757537.	9	1.282	28.2	−21.6
Kansas	2178611.	7	1.263	26.3	−22.8
Ky.	3038156.	9	1.164	16.4	−28.8
La.	3257022.	10	1.206	20.6	−26.2
Maine	969265.	4	1.622	62.2	−.8
Md.	3100689.	10	1.267	26.7	−22.5
Mass.	5148578.	14	1.068	6.8	−34.7
Mich.	7823194.	21	1.055	5.5	−35.5
Minn.	3413864.	10	1.151	15.1	−29.6
Miss.	2178141.	7	1.263	26.3	−22.8

State Name (1)	Population 1960 Census	Electoral Vote 1968	Relative Voting Power (2)	Percent Excess Voting Power (3)	Percent Deviation From Average Voting Power (4)
Mo.	4319813.	12	1.092	9.2	−33.3
Mont.	674767.	4	2.329	132.9	42.4
Neb.	1411330.	5	1.392	39.2	−14.9
Nev.	285278.	3	4.132	313.2	152.7
N. H.	606921.	4	2.590	159.0	58.3
N. J.	6066782.	17	1.101	10.1	−32.7
N. M.	951023.	4	1.653	65.3	1.1
N. Y.	16782304.	43	1.007	.7	−38.4
N. C.	4556155.	13	1.121	12.1	−31.4
N. D.	632446.	4	2.485	148.5	52.0
Ohio	9706397.	26	1.053	5.3	−35.6
Okla.	2328284.	8	1.350	35.0	−17.4
Ore.	1768687	6	1.333	33.3	−18.5
Penn.	11319366.	29	1.007	.7	−38.4
R. I.	859488.	4	1.829	82.9	11.8
S. C.	2382594.	8	1.319	31.9	−19.3
S. D.	680514.	4	2.310	131.0	41.2
Tenn.	3567089.	11	1.212	21.2	−25.9
Texas	9579677.	25	1.025	2.5	−37.3
Utah	890627.	4	1.765	76.5	7.9
Vt.	389881.	3	3.023	202.3	84.9
Va.	3966949.	12	1.189	18.9	−27.3
Wash.	2853214.	9	1.239	23.9	−24.2
W. V.	1860421.	7	1.478	47.8	−9.6
Wis.	3951777.	12	1.193	19.3	−27.0
Wyo.	330066.	3	3.571	257.1	118.4

(1) Includes the District of Columbia.
(2) Ratio of voting power of citizens of state compared with voters of the most deprived state.
(3) Percent by which voting power exceeds that of the most deprived voters (deviations).
(4) Percent by which voting power deviated from the average of the figures in column 4.
Minus signs indicate less than average voting power.

3. THE DISTRICT PLAN

State Name (1)	Population 1960 Census	Electoral Vote 1968	Relative Voting Power (2)	Percent Excess Voting Power (3)	Percent Deviation From Average Voting Power (4)
Ala.	3266740.	10	1.302	30.2	—15.7
Alaska	226167.	3	3.075	207.5	99.1
Ariz.	1302161.	5	1.594	59.4	3.2
Ark.	1786272.	6	1.459	45.9	—5.5
Calif.	15717204.	40	1.004	.4	—35.0
Colo.	1753947.	6	1.472	47.2	—4.7
Conn.	2535234.	8	1.362	36.2	—11.8
Del.	446292.	3	2.189	118.9	41.7
D. C.	763956.	3	1.673	67.3	8.3
Fla.	4951560.	14	1.197	19.7	—22.5
Ga.	3943116.	12	1.267	26.7	—18.0
Hawaii	632772.	4	2.092	109.2	35.5
Idaho	667191.	4	2.038	103.8	31.9
Ill.	10081158.	26	1.059	5.9	—31.4
Ind.	4662498.	13	1.200	20.0	—22.3
Iowa	2757537.	9	1.364	36.4	—11.7
Kansas	2178611.	7	1.399	39.9	—9.4
Ky.	3038156.	9	1.299	29.9	—15.9
La.	3257022.	10	1.304	30.4	—15.6
Maine	969265.	4	1.691	69.1	9.4
Md.	3100689.	10	1.337	33.7	—13.5
Mass.	5148578.	14	1.174	17.4	—24.0
Mich.	7823194.	21	1.108	10.8	—28.3
Minn.	3413864.	10	1.274	27.4	—17.5
Miss.	2178141.	7	1.399	39.9	—9.4

State Name (1)	Population 1960 Census	Electoral Vote 1968	Relative Voting Power (2)	Percent Excess Voting Power (3)	Percent Deviation From Average Voting Power (4)
Mo.	4319813.	12	1.211	21.1	—21.6
Mont.	674767.	4	2.026	102.6	31.2
Neb.	1411330.	5	1.532	53.2	—.9
Nev.	285278.	3	2.738	173.8	77.3
N. H.	606921.	4	2.137	113.7	38.3
N. J.	6066782.	17	1.162	16.2	—24.7
N. M.	951023.	4	1.707	70.7	10.5
N. Y.	16782304.	43	1.000	.0	—35.3
N. C.	4556155.	13	1.214	21.4	—21.4
N. D.	632446.	4	2.093	109.3	35.5
Ohio	9706397.	26	1.080	8.0	—30.1
Okla.	2328284.	8	1.422	42.2	—8.0
Ore.	1768687	6	1.466	46.6	—5.1
Penn.	11319366.	29	1.043	4.3	—32.5
R. I.	859488.	4	1.795	79.5	16.2
S. C.	2382594.	8	1.405	40.5	—9.0
S. D.	680514.	4	2.018	101.8	30.6
Tenn.	3567089.	11	1.291	29.1	—16.5
Texas	9579677.	25	1.070	7.0	—30.7
Utah	890627.	4	1.764	76.4	14.2
Vt.	389881.	3	2.342	134.2	51.6
Va.	3966949.	12	1.264	26.4	—18.2
Wash.	2853214.	9	1.341	34.1	—13.2
W. Va.	1860421.	7	1.514	51.4	—2.0
Wis.	3951777.	12	1.266	26.6	—18.0
Wyo.	330066.	3	2.546	154.6	64.8

(1) Includes the District of Columbia.

(2) Ratio of voting power of citizens of state compared with voters of the most deprived state.

(3) Percent by which voting power exceeds that of the most deprived voters (deviations).

(4) Percent by which voting power deviated from the average of the figures in column 4.

Minus signs indicate less than average voting power.

4. DIRECT POPULAR VOTE

State Name	Population 1960 Census	Population 1970 Estimate (1)	Electoral Vote 1968
Alabama	3266740.	3,670,000	10
Alaska	226167.	298,000	3
Arizona	1302161.	1,828,000	5
Arkansas	1786272.	2,053,000	6
California	15717204.	21,004,000	40
Colorado	1753947.	2,124,000	6
Connecticut	2535234.	3,088,000	8
Delaware	446292.	555,000	3
Dist. of Columbia	763956.	852,000	3
Florida	4951560.	6,654,000	14
Georgia	3943116.	4,741,000	12
Hawaii	632772.	763,000	4
Idaho	667191.	717,000	4
Illinois	10081158.	11,115,000	26
Indiana	4662498.	5,095,000	13
Iowa	2757537.	2,748,000	9
Kansas	2178611.	2,304,000	7
Kentucky	3038156.	3,265,000	9
Louisiana	3257022.	3,819,000	10
Maine	969265.	998,000	4
Maryland	3100689.	3,915,000	10
Massachusetts	5148578.	5,544,000	14
Michigan	7823194.	8,706,000	21
Minnesota	3413864.	3,684,000	10
Mississippi	2178141.	2,413,000	7

(1) This column added to Banzhaf study for purposes of comparison.

Electoral Vote 1972 Estimate (1)	Relative Voting Power	Percent Excess Voting Power	Percent Deviation From Average Voting Power
10	1.000	0.0	0.0
3	1.000	0.0	0.0
6 +	1.000	0.0	0.0
6	1.000	0.0	0.0
46 +	1.000	0.0	0.0
6	1.000	0.0	0.0
8	1.000	0.0	0.0
3	1.000	0.0	0.0
3	1.000	0.0	0.0
16 +	1.000	0.0	0.0
12	1.000	0.0	0.0
4	1.000	0.0	0.0
4	1.000	0.0	0.0
25 −	1.000	0.0	0.0
13	1.000	0.0	0.0
8 −	1.000	0.0	0.0
7	1.000	0.0	0.0
9	1.000	0.0	0.0
10	1.000	0.0	0.0
4	1.000	0.0	0.0
10	1.000	0.0	0.0
14	1.000	0.0	0.0
20 −	1.000	0.0	0.0
10	1.000	0.0	0.0
7	1.000	0.0	0.0

State Name	Population 1960 Census	Population 1970 Estimate (1)	Electoral Vote 1968
Missouri	4319813.	4,636,000	12
Montana	674767.	725,000	4
Nebraska	1411330.	1,486,000	5
Nevada	285278.	547,000	3
New Hampshire	606921.	731,000	4
New Jersey	6066782.	7,411,000	17
New Mexico	951023.	1,091,000	4
New York	16782304.	19,157,000	43
North Carolina	4556155.	5,232,000	13
North Dakota	632446.	659,000	4
Ohio	9706397.	10,721,000	26
Oklahoma	2328284.	2,536,000	8
Oregon	1768687.	2,076,000	6
Pennsylvania	11319366.	11,758,000	29
Rhode Island	859488.	920,000	4
South Carolina	2382594.	2,689,000	8
South Dakota	680514.	686,000	4
Tennessee	3567089.	4,072,000	11
Texas	9579677.	11,452,000	25
Utah	890627.	1,087,000	4
Vermont	389881.	418,000	3
Virginia	3966949.	4,806,000	12
Washington	2853214.	3,098,000	9
West Virginia	1860421.	1,766,000	7
Wisconsin	3951777.	4,296,000	12
Wyoming	330066.	335,000	3

(1) This column added to Banzhaf study for purposes of comparison.

Electoral Vote 1972 Estimate (1)	Relative Voting Power	Percent Excess Voting Power	Percent Deviation From Average Voting Power
12	1.000	0.0	0.0
4	1.000	0.0	0.0
5	1.000	0.0	0.0
3	1.000	0.0	0.0
4	1.000	0.0	0.0
18 +	1.000	0.0	0.0
4	1.000	0.0	0.0
42 −	1.000	0.0	0.0
13	1.000	0.0	0.0
3 −	1.000	0.0	0.0
25 −	1.000	0.0	0.0
7 −	1.000	0.0	0.0
6	1.000	0.0	0.0
27 −	1.000	0.0	0.0
4	1.000	0.0	0.0
8	1.000	0.0	0.0
4	1.000	0.0	0.0
11	1.000	0.0	0.0
26 +	1.000	0.0	0.0
4	1.000	0.0	0.0
3	1.000	0.0	0.0
12	1.000	0.0	0.0
9	1.000	0.0	0.0
6 −	1.000	0.0	0.0
11 −	1.000	0.0	0.0
3	1.000	0.0	0.0

APPENDIX D

1968 PRESIDENTIAL ELECTION RESULTS

State	Electoral Vote	Nixon	Pct.	Humphrey	Pct.	Wallace
Ala.	10	146,923	14.1	194,388	18.6	689,009
Alaska	3	37,540	45.2	35,411	42.7	10,024
Ariz.	5	266,721	54.8	170,514	35.0	46,573
Ark.	6	189,062	31.0	184,901	30.3	235,627
Calif.	40	3,467,644	47.8	3,244,318	44.7	487,270
Colo.	6	409,345	50.8	331,063	41.0	60,813
Conn.	8	556,721	44.4	621,561	49.5	76,650
Del.	3	96,714	45.1	89,194	41.6	28,459
D. C.	3	31,012	18.2	139,556	81.8	—
Fla.	14	886,804	40.5	676,794	30.9	624,207
Ga.	12	366,611	29.7	334,439	27.0	535,550
Hawaii	4	91,425	38.7	141,324	59.8	3,469
Idaho	4	165,369	56.8	89,273	30.7	36,541
Ill.	26	2,174,774	47.1	2,039,814	44.2	390,958
Ind.	13	1,067,885	50.3	806,659	38.0	243,108
Iowa	9	619,106	53.0	476,699	40.8	66,422
Kans.	7	478,674	54.8	302,996	34.7	88,921
Ky.	9	462,411	43.8	397,541	37.6	193,098
La.	10	257,535	23.5	309,615	28.2	530,300
Maine	4	169,254	43.1	217,312	55.3	6,370
Md.	10	517,995	41.9	538,310	43.6	178,734
Mass.	14	766,844	32.9	1,469,218	63.0	87,088
Mich.	21	1,370,665	41.5	1,593,082	48.2	331,968
Minn.	10	658,643	41.5	857,738	54.0	68,931
Miss.	7	88,516	13.5	150,644	23.0	415,349

Pct.	Others	Pct.	Plurality		State	N	Electoral Vote H	W
66.0	13,857	1.3	494,621	W	Ala.			10
12.1	—	—	2,129	N	Alaska	3		
9.6	3,128	.6	96,207	N	Ariz.	5		
38.7	—	—	46,565	W	Ark.			6
6.8	52,335	.7	223,326	N	Calif.	40		
7.5	5,762	.7	78,282	N	Colo.	6		
6.1	—	—	64,840	H	Conn.		8	
13.3	—	—	7,520	N	Del.	3		
—	—	—	108,544	H	D.C.		3	
28.6	—	—	210,010	N	Fla.	14		
43.3	—	—	168,939	W	Ga.			12
1.5	—	—	49,899	H	Hawaii		4	
12.5	—	—	76,096	N	Idaho	4		
8.5	13,878	.2	134,960	N	Ill.	26		
11.4	5,909	.3	261,226	N	Ind.	13		
5.7	5,704	.5	142,407	N	Iowa	9		
10.2	2,192	.3	175,678	N	Kans.	7		
18.3	2,843	.3	64,870	N	Ky.	9		
48.3	—	—	220,685	W	La.			10
1.6	—	—	48,058	H	Maine		4	
14.5	—	—	20,315	H	Md.		10	
3.7	8,602	.4	702,374	H	Mass.		14	
10.0	10,535	.3	222,417	H	Mich.		21	
4.3	3,198	.2	199,095	H	Minn.		10	
63.5	—	—	264,705	W	Miss.			7

State	Electoral Vote	Nixon	Pct.	Humphrey	Pct.	Wallace
Mo.	12	811,932	44.9	791,444	43.7	206,126
Mont.	4	138,853	50.6	114,117	41.6	20,015
Neb.	5	321,163	59.8	170,784	31.8	44,904
Nev.	3	73,188	47.5	60,598	39.3	20,432
N. H.	4	154,903	52.1	130,589	43.9	11,173
N. J.	17	1,325,467	46.1	1,264,206	44.0	262,187
N. M.	4	169,692	51.8	130,081	39.7	25,737
N. Y.	43	3,007,938	44.3	3,378,470	49.8	358,864
N. C.	13	627,192	39.5	464,113	29.2	496,188
N. D.	4	138,669	55.9	94,769	38.2	14,244
Ohio	26	1,791,014	45.2	1,700,586	42.9	467,495
Okla.	8	449,697	47.4	306,658	32.3	191,731
Ore.	6	408,433	49.8	358,865	43.8	49,683
Pa.	29	2,090,017	43.9	2,259,403	47.5	387,582
R. I.	4	122,359	31.8	246,518	64.0	15,678
S. C.	8	254,062	38.1	197,486	29.6	215,430
S. D.	4	149,841	53.3	118,023	42.0	13,400
Tenn.	11	472,592	37.8	351,233	28.1	424,792
Texas	25	1,227,844	39.9	1,266,804	41.1	584,269
Utah	4	238,728	56.5	156,665	37.1	26,906
Vt.	3	85,142	52.8	70,255	43.5	5,104
Va.	12	590,315	43.4	442,387	32.5	320,272
Wash.	9	588,510	45.1	616,037	47.2	72,560
W. Va.	7	307,555	40.8	374,091	49.6	72,560
Wis.	12	809,997	47.9	748,804	44.3	127,835
Wyo.	3	70,927	55.8	45,173	35.5	11,105
Totals		31,770,237	43.4	31,270,533	42.7	9,906,141

Pct.	Others	Pct.	Plurality	State	Electoral Vote N	H	W
11.4	—	—	20,488 N	Mo.	12		
7.3	1,437	.5	24,736 N	Mont.	4		
8.4	—	—	150,379 N	Neb.	5		
13.2	—	—	12,590 N	Nev.	3		
3.8	535	.2	24,314 N	N. H.	4		
9.1	23,536	.8	61,261 N	N. J.	17		
7.9	1,771	.6	39,611 N	N. M.	4		
5.3	44,800	.6	370,532 H	N. Y.		43	
31.3	—	—	131,004 N	N. C.	12		1
5.7	200	.2	43,900 N	N. D.	4		
11.8	603	.1	90,428 N	Ohio	26		
20.3	—	—	143,039 N	Okla.	8		
6.1	2,640	.3	49,568 N	Ore.	6		
8.1	19,922	.5	169,386 H	Pa.		29	
4.1	383	.1	124,159 H	R. I.		4	
32.3	—	—	38,632 N	S. C.	8		
4.7	—	—	31,818 N	S. D.	4		
34.1	—	—	47,800 N	Tenn.	11		
19.0	489	—	38,960 H	Texas		25	
6.4	180	—	82,063 N	Utah	4		
3.2	873	.5	14,887 N	Vt.	3		
23.6	6,950	.5	147,928 N	Va.	12		
9.6	—	—	27,527 H	Wash.		9	
9.6	—	—	66,536 H	W. Va.		7	
7.6	4,902	.2	61,193 N	Wis.	12		
8.7	—	—	25,754 N	Wyo.	3		
13.5	239,908	.4	499,704 N		301	191	46

APPENDIX E

PENNSYLVANIA
ELECTORAL COLLEGE
PROCEDURE

The Order of Business to be followed at the convening of the electors on Monday, December 16, 1968, at 12:00 o'clock noon in the Hall of the House of Representatives in Harrisburg will be as follows:

1. Call to order by the Secretary of the Commonwealth
2. Invocation
3. Address by Secretary of the Commonwealth
4. Appointment of temporary officers by the Secretary of the Commonwealth (Parliamentarian, Secretary, Sergeant-at-Arms)
5. Communications presented from Governor regarding certified lists of persons elected at General Election which are tabled
6. Resolution presented to have communications read
7. Communications taken from table and read
8. Roll call of electors
9. Resolution presented requesting a Judge to administer oath of office to electors
10. Oath administered
11. Election of a President of the Electoral College (by resolution)
12. Address by President

13. Announcement of electors who did not answer when roll was called
14. Resolution to fill vacancies in electoral college (if any)
15. Resolution to notify Governor of action taken to fill vacancies (if any)
16. Communication from Governor acknowledging receipt of notification regarding filling of vacancies (if any)
17. Oath administered to electors elected by the college to fill vacancies (if any)
18. Election of a Vice President by resolution
19. Permanent officers appointed by resolution (Secretary, Parliamentarian, Chief Sergeant-at-Arms, Stenographic Reporter, Chief Page and Page
20. Resolution regarding procedures (the procedure usually follows the preceding college)
21. Resolution authorizing the President of the Electoral College to appoint a committee to inform the Governor that the Electoral College is organized and to invite him to address the college
22. Introduction of distinguished guests (if any)
23. Committee to inform Governor reports and escorts Governor to the college
24. Address by Governor
25. Committee escorts Governor to his office
26. Resolution to proceed to ballot for President of the United States
27. Appointment of tellers (3) by the President of the Electoral College
28. Balloting for President of the United States One ballot for President of the United States is distributed by the tellers to each elector. Each elector writes the name of the person whom he or she votes for the Office of President of the United States on the ballot. As the secretary calls the name of the elector he or she comes forward and deposits his or her ballot in the ballot box, marked with the name of his or her choice for President of the United States.
29. Report of balloting by tellers to the President of the Electoral College
30. President of the Electoral College announces results of balloting for President of the United States

31. President of the Electoral College asks Vice President of the Electoral College to preside during balloting for Vice President of the United States

32. Address by Vice President of the Electoral College

33. Balloting for Vice President of the United States (same procedure as for President of the United States)

34. Report of balloting by tellers to the Vice President of the Electoral College

35. Vice President of the Electoral College announces the result of the balloting for Vice President of the United States

36. Signing of Certificate of Election of President and Vice President of the United States by the electors
    Six certificates of election are placed on a table in the front of the Hall of the House of Representatives. As the secretary calls the roll each elector comes to the front of the House and signs the six certificates. The disposition of these certificates are explained later.

37. Resolution for appointment of a committee to see that the list of Electors and certificates of votes cast for President and Vice President of the United States are enclosed in separate envelopes and that each is sealed, directed, certified and signed.

38. Resolution appointing one of the electors to take in charge one of the packages containing one list of the Electors originally elected, one certificate of the election filling vacancies in the Electoral College, if any, and one certificate of the votes cast for President and Vice President of the United States, directed to the President of the United States Senate in Washington, D. C., by delivering the same to the Postmaster at the City of Harrisburg, and to have the same registered and mailed.

39. Resolution appointing one of the electors to take in charge one of the packages containing two lists of the Electors originally elected, two certificates of the election filling vacancies in the Electoral College, if any, and two certificates of the votes cast for President and Vice President of the United States, to be delivered to the Secretary of the Commonwealth, one of which shall be held subject to the order of the President of the United States Senate, the other to be preserved by the Secretary of the Commonwealth for one year and shall be

a part of the public records of his office and shall be open to public inspection. The resolution also provides for the filing of the proceedings of the Electoral College with the Secretary of the Commonwealth.

40. Resolution appointing one of the Electors to take in charge one package containing two lists of Electors originally elected, two certificates of election filling vacancies in the Electoral College, if any, and two certificates of the votes cast for President and Vice President of the United States, which shall be forwarded by registered mail, through the Postmaster of Harrisburg, to the Administrator of General Services of the United States on the day following the meeting of the Electoral College.

41. Resolution appointing one of the Electors to take in charge one package containing one list of the electors originally selected, one certificate of the election filling vacancies in the electoral college, if any, and one certificate of the votes cast for the President and Vice President of the United States, and forward the same by registered mail through the Postmaster at Harrisburg, to the Chief Judge of the District Court of the United States for the Middle District of Pennsylvania.

42. President of the Electoral College requests the persons appointed pursuant to the foregoing resolutions dealing with the disposition of the certificates to meet immediately after adjournment with the Secretary and Assistant Secretary for further instructions

43. Resolution appointing three Electors as a Committee on Accounts and Expenses

44. Resolution ordering the publication of the proceedings of the Electoral College. Said publication to be delivered to and distributed by the Secretary of the Commonwealth

45. Resolution thanking the officers of the College

46. Closing remarks by the President of the Electoral College

47. Resolution for adjournment

48. Benediction

49. Adjournment

If the certificate of electoral votes is not received by the President of the United States Senate or by the Administrator of General Services by the fourth Wednesday in December after the meeting of the state's electors, this falling on Christmas Day this year, the President of the United States Senate or, in his absence, the Administrator of General Services must ask the Secretary of the Commonwealth to send these documents. Upon receipt of such request, the Secretary of the Commonwealth must immediately transmit the documents to the President of the United States Senate in Washington.

When the President of the U. S. Senate or the Administrator of General Services makes his request to the Secretary of the Commonwealth, he (the President of the U. S. Senate or the Administrator of General Services) must also send a special messenger to the district judge, who has custody of one certificate of the votes. The district judge must forthwith give that certificate to the messenger.

JAMES A. MICHENER, one of the world's most popular writers, was the author of the Pulitzer Prize–winning *Tales of the South Pacific,* the best-selling novels *Hawaii, Texas, Chesapeake, The Covenant,* and *Alaska,* and the memoir *The World Is My Home.* Michener served on the advisory council to NASA and the International Broadcast Board, which oversees the Voice of America. Among dozens of awards and honors, he received America's highest civilian award, the Presidential Medal of Freedom, in 1977, and an award from the President's Committee on the Arts and Humanities in 1983 for his commitment to art in America. Michener died in 1997 at the age of ninety.

ABOUT THE TYPE

This book was set in Times Roman, designed by Stanley Morison (1889–1967) specifically for *The Times* of London. The typeface was introduced in the newspaper in 1932. Times Roman had its greatest success in the United States as a book and commercial typeface, rather than one used in newspapers.